# THE LAND THAT NEVER WAS

M

*Alyse Simpson*

# THE LAND THAT NEVER WAS

University of Nebraska Press
Lincoln and London

Copyright 1937 by Selwyn & Blount
Foreword copyright 1985 by the University of Nebraska Press
All rights reserved
Manufactured in the United States of America

First Bison Book printing: June 1985
Most recent printing indicated by the first digit below:
1    2    3    4    5    6    7    8    9    10

Library of Congress Cataloging in Publication Data
Simpson, Alyse.
    The land that never was.
    Reprint. Originally published: London: Selwyn &
Blount, 1937.
    1. Simpson, Alyse. 2. Kenya—Social life and
customs—1895–1963. 3. Country life—Kenya—History—
20th century. 4. British—Kenya—Biography. I. Title.
DT433.576.S55A34 1985      967.6'203      84-27998
ISBN 0-8032-4149-6
ISBN 0-8032-9146-9 (pbk.)

Reprinted by arrangement with Hutchinson Publishing Group
Limited, London

# Foreword
## By Dane Kennedy

"The land that never was" refers to colonial Kenya, a realm of extravagant reputation. Proclaimed a British protectorate in 1895, this East African territory soon attracted a steady stream of white settlers from South Africa and especially the United Kingdom. By the interwar years the colony had acquired renown as one of the most grand and enchanting stars in Britain's imperial galaxy. A sizable travel and promotional literature, supplemented by romantic novels and newspaper stories, portrayed Kenya as an exotic paradise, blessed with a mild and sunny climate, a profusion of big game, a landscape of spectacular beauty, and a virtually inexhaustible supply of cheap native labor. Here, so it seemed, the white population was composed mainly of self-exiled aristocrats and retired army officers who led lives of affluent leisure, spiced with scandal and adventure. It is this overwrought reputation that Alyse Simpson seeks to controvert in her aptly titled memoir.

Her tale is one of disillusionment, providing a revealing and valuable corrective to the roseate popular image of the white settler's experience in Kenya. With cool candor, Simpson recounts how her husband and she failed as settlers in the colony. They were not alone. The simple fact is that many of those whom hyperbolic promises had brought to East Africa found it to be a harsh, alien, unpredictable land, and they remigrated in surprising numbers. Customs data indicate that for every ten persons who entered Kenya in the interwar years, nine departed. Not all did so embittered and impoverished like the Simpsons, of course, but Alyse's story is representative of a significant and otherwise silent segment of this exceedingly inconstant white settler population.

# FOREWORD

Why did the Simpsons risk their life savings on this venture in a strange land of uncertain potential? Their motives were not untypical of British immigrants to Kenya—nor, for that matter, of European settlers in other colonized territories. The beguiling claims for East Africa's promise, particularly when articulated by a cousin in the country, were doubtless instrumental in their decision, but it seems probable that had Kenya not caught their attention, Southern Rhodesia or Canada or another land would have done so. The major impetus came not from abroad but from home. The author alludes to a complex array of factors: above all the desire to improve upon the stagnant economic opportunities to be had in industrial England, but also the dissatisfaction with the social constraints and conventions of their native land, the shame of their failures as measured by critical relatives, the restlessness over the lack of "freedom" and "adventure" in their lives, even the vague discontent with England's damp and dreary climate. These motives were shared in varied proportions by most other emigrants from Britain, and they made the task of pioneering a new territory not only acceptable but attractive.

Yet an imposing task it was. In the interwar era when the Simpsons came to Kenya, even the most optimistic authorities recommended a minimum capital of £2,000 for new settlers; the more frequently quoted figure was £4,000–5,000. Financial requirements were far greater for farmers intending to develop virgin land. To judge from these estimates, the Simpsonses' £2,000 was simply inadequate for their thousand acres of unworked and untested soil. Such undercapitalization was a common problem in the settler community, and helps account for widespread indebtedness. What made large infusions of capital necessary were the continual uncertainties of commercial agriculture in the colony. For a start, new arrivals were often woefully ignorant of such vital matters as what crops would grow on their land, particularly if they came from the sort of urban, commercial background exemplified by the Simpsons. Even the accrual of experience offered little redress for such unpredictable natural depredations as drought, disease, and locusts. Nor could personal initiative prevent those vagaries of the international market system that caused disaster for Kenya's agricultural economy in the early 1920s and through most of the 1930s. In such circumstances, the settlers with the best hopes of survival were those least dependent upon turning a profit from agriculture, and it is significant in this respect that a very high percentage of the colony's white community consisted of former government and professional careerists who drew regular revenue from pensions, stocks, and bonds.

The Simpsons, however, lacked an outside income, and they went under. This central fact infuses the author's narrative with a candor that is absent from most other works of this genre. It is not so much the description of physical hardships which distinguishes the book—many settler memoirs chew that subject with relish—but rather the sober portrait it paints of colonial society. The miscellaneous collection of dispirited and temperamental colonists who people these pages seem joined by little more than their economic tribulations and their racial paramountcy. Although this view is certainly colored by the author's bitter feelings, it contributes a truth that the sunny stereotypes neglect. Perhaps because Alyse Simpson has left Kenya, she feels no obligations in recounting her story to conform to the ideological and attitudinal norms of the white settler community. One of the most contented and sympathetic individuals she meets in the colony is an eccentric English gentleman who has "gone native," converting to Islam and living a peripatetic existence. Such behavior, so at odds with the social standards expected of white colonists, was regarded with intense disfavor by most settlers—but not by Alyse. The greatest danger she encounters during her years on an isolated Kenya homestead comes not from "savage" Africans—though she expresses some initial fears of that kind—but from a drunken and violent European. Significantly, she is saved by her black cook. The Africans as a whole are portrayed with uncommon sympathy and respect. To be sure, Alyse Simpson adopts the conventional view that the African people are happy creatures with no care for the future, but she expresses none of the sour, impatient, hostile feelings toward black servants and laborers that pervade most settler memoirs. Her narrative is peppered with censorious accounts of various cruelties, ranging from financial fraud to physical beatings inflicted on African employees by their European masters. This critical perspective on race relations is perhaps the most accurate measure of the author's distance from the rigorously enforced norms of the settler community.

Is it any wonder, then, that Simpson takes pains to disguise the subjects of her story? Her hometown of Mannington, the Kenyan hamlet of Nymba, the Simba valley that contains her farm, the Kamasia people who live in a nearby reserve, and presumably the names of the main characters are all pseudonyms. The geographical and ecological details are ambiguous and sometimes contradictory. Even the precise years of her Kenyan adventure are obscure. Assuming, as I think one must, that the author practiced this dissimulation for sensitive personal reasons can only add further poignancy to her unhappy tale.

Although the particular milieu of this book is the settler society of interwar Kenya, from a broader perspective it offers insight into the experience of women in frontier environments. The circumstances described by Alyse Simpson suggest clear parallels to those faced by pioneer women in the American West. On both frontiers, many women struggled to establish homes and families in primitive conditions, braving a raw and unfamiliar land in rude dwellings with the barest of amenities. Confronted by illness, accidents, and pregnancy, they seldom could depend upon the assistance of trained doctors. The monotony and loneliness of frontier life frequently told on their mental health. Whether situated in the East African highlands or the American prairies, frontier women were necessarily reliant on their own resources to a great extent, and they responded to the challenge in accord with their own varied characters.

In one important respect, however, the experience of Simpson and other settler women in Kenya differed radically from that of their counterparts in America. It is evident that the author had the abundant services of Africans to do the cooking

FOREWORD

and other domestic chores, as her husband did for farm work. This was typically the case for white settlers in Kenya, no matter how insolvent their finances. The result was a degree of leisure and freedom from drudgery that women of the American frontier, where the American Indians remained aloof and labor scarce, could hardly have imagined. Whether the settler women of Kenya were the enviable party is perhaps more problematical than cursory consideration might suggest. If Alysé Simpson's experience is any indication, the extended leisure available to Kenya's white women probably accentuated the psychological burdens of loneliness and boredom. Moreover, in contrast to the liberating qualities which some scholars argue that the demands of frontier life brought to women in the American West, the less physical and more ladylike lifestyle of Kenyan females may well have sustained traditional social constraints on their roles and responsibilities.

Readers of this book are sure to draw further insights of their own. For this is an exceptional memoir—sensitive in its perceptions, independent in its perspective, honest in its judgments. If Alyse Simpson's Kenyan venture was a failure in the eyes of her neighbors in the colony and her family in England, the chronicle it conceived is quite the contrary: it does much to enrich our understanding of the settler experience.

## Glossary

**Lincolnshire** (p. 14): a county in England
**topee** (p. 19): a pith helmet used by British in tropical colonies to protect them from solar rays
**Mezuri sana** (p. 23): Swahili for "very nice" or "fine"; commonly spelled *mzuri sana*
**Swahili** (p. 23): an African people native to the East African coast of Kenya; also the trade language of Eastern Africa, a mixture of Arabic and Bantu
**Kavirondo** (p. 32): colonial term for the Luo and neighboring peoples who occupy the area around the Kavirondo Gulf in western Kenya

ix

FOREWORD

**rickshaw** (p. 32): the major form of transport within the city of Nairobi until the introduction of the automobile

**Lake Victoria Nyanza** (p. 46): commonly known as Lake Victoria, the largest lake in the East African chain

**Goanese clerk** (p. 49): from the Portuguese colony of Goa on the west coast of India; many Goanese came to Kenya to serve as functionaries in the colonial government and other middle-level occupations

**Uganda railway** (p. 54): major railway through Kenya, stretching from Mombasa on the Indian Ocean to Kisumu on Lake Victoria's shores, constructed from 1896 to 1902

**Masai** (p. 61): a pastoral people who live in the Rift Valley and surrounding territory of Kenya and Tanzania

**Kikuyu country** (p. 72): central Kenyan highlands, populated by the Kikuyu people, but much of it taken by white settlers

**Vaderobos** (p. 78): properly termed Dorobo or Okick, a hunter-gatherer people who live in isolated bands in the forest areas of central Kenya

**Laikipia** (p. 90): a plateau northwest of the Rift Valley

**Askari** (p. 105): Swahili term for African policeman or soldier

**Aberdares** (p. 156): a range of mountains north of Nairobi

**Lake Rudolf** (p. 167): a lake in northern Kenya

**Lake Baringo** (p. 199): a lake in the northern Rift Valley of Kenya

**Mount Kenya** (p. 237): the highest mountain in Kenya

The following names and terms are, I am relatively certain, fictitious:

**Mannington**
**Nymba** (p. 36)
**Simba valley** (p. 40)
**Naituka** (p. 54)
**Kamasias** (p. 80)
**Simba swamp** (p. 166)

# THE LAND THAT NEVER WAS

# THE LAND THAT NEVER WAS

THIS NARRATIVE OF LIFE IN KENYA HAS BEEN WRITTEN FOR those light-hearted people, young and old, who even in these days still dream of some distant Eldorado to which they can flee from a chaotic world. But if the book " damps the ardour " of the aforementioned light-hearted people, it certainly will not bore them. . . .

In one sense, perhaps, *The Land that Never Was* may be described as heart-breaking, yet it is also both exciting and absorbing, for it is the record of the adventures—and the eventual disillusionment of ideals—of a very young married couple who, lured by the idea of freedom and open spaces, " took the plunge " and sought fortune in the sunny land of Kenya. With them they took £2000 and an immense hope ; and having at length found and purchased a small farm, they set out on the Great Adventure by growing coffee and maize.

The simple, straightforward and honest account of all that happened embodies this book. It is a record of fact, shorn of all embellishments and related without self-pity—a true record of first-hand experience that is told in a curiously artless style which really does grip the imagination and tempt the reader to read on in order to know how the Great Adventure ended.

Much has been written about the delights of sunny Kenya and the land of fortune that it is. The author's story gives—without bitterness—the other side of the picture, and *it is packed with information which a large public ought to know.*

The charm of the author's style holds a fascination all its own ; whilst comedy, tragedy and thrills (whether they be marauding wild animals, plagues of locusts, the antics of the native cook or the stark reality of inevitable bankruptcy . . .) jostle one another and lure the reader into complete absorption in the author's story.

# I

It was a chilly day in october, some years ago now, when John and I sailed out to Kenya.

There were a couple of small trunks down in the hold of the ship, and a cheque for two thousand pounds in John's pocket. These were all our earthly possessions. One of the trunks contained a rifle, a shotgun, and a ·22, a revolver, a medicine-chest and some crockery. The other one was filled with khaki clothes. It was completely against all commonsense to go, and I still wonder no one tried to stop us. Heaven knows, we had been interfered with enough since we were children by well-meaning parents. It had even been hinted by a series of successful uncles and other closer, but equally light-hearted relations, that Kenya would indeed be a good " way out." " Out of what ? " I have asked myself since. . . .

There was a promise of wealth in the air—and of adventure. No one could have stopped us really, even had they tried. John had always been a dreamer, ready to pack his bag and burn his boats behind him at the slightest provocation. Woman-like, I was more of a realist at heart, but then I was ashamed of that. Remembering the need for courage and probable discomforts at the time when John spoke romantically of freedom, somehow seemed all wrong. Had anyone told us that the chances of profitable farming in Kenya were small, we should not, I expect,

5

have believed them. We were going to make good ; it was also expected of us.

Now that it is all over and we are back at home again after nearly six years in the wilds, I will try to describe our adventure. Clearly I recollect every incident, and am amazed how very much alert we were at the time—in spite of having frequently been laid so low by the climate. I shall not, I hope, commit the unforgivable sin of encouraging other similar young lunatics with insufficient capital to go out to Kenya in search of wealth or romance. Enough of this sort of bunkum has been written. Kenya is a cruel country, if the truth be told ; but alas, men like John do not write books. . . .

The everyday task of a pioneer on the Equator, his Sisyphean labour, will not encourage him to talk about himself ; like the soldier back from the war or the sailor back from the sea, he will keep silent. It is not he who will tell you of this distant Eldorado. Let others write of giant elephant-hunts, of facing charging lions and rhinoceros, or of the love-life of the natives and other interesting facts. His concern from day to day is, " will it rain soon ? ; will the ' fly ' get the coffee ? ; will the locusts come this way ? ; shall I have to write home for more money ? ; or shall I keep within the limits of my overdraft ? " He cannot ease his burden by leaning over the garden gate in the pleasant cool of the evening, discussing his day's work with a neighbour. John's diary, his only attempt at any kind of writing, was merely a sort of log.

The things nearest at heart were entered, but there was no poetry there. Facts, facts, and fears between the lines. Rain or no rain, that was the question— it was the everlasting question of his life. A few other items coloured the pages of his daily records. " Pigs eaten by sow " ; " mule died of horse sickness " ;

" ox blown by new green grass, dead " ; " two more oxen blown, dead." " X. called, stayed a week." What an event it was, the rare sight of another White man. Even the most atrocious bore was welcome ! Trembling I would run into my bedroom at the approach of a visitor, to collect myself before I dared venture forth to greet the new-comer. Powdering my nose, I rehearsed some sentences, for I had lost the gift of small talk. . . .

Having spent five dreary years in Mannington, a city in the Midlands, which used to be a very prosperous manufacturing town before the war, John and I had failed to make what we then considered a decent living, so we set out upon our voyage to Kenya. After we had sold everything we owned—house, furniture and small car—we had exactly two thousand pounds. Ample, we were told by people who should have known better. Theoretically, it was enough. But farming on paper does not allow for those surprises that Kenya has in store for young hopefuls which dash their spirits and claim their money.

" Come to Kenya,"—thus ran an advertisement which had helped to change our lives and which had held forth new hopes and conjured images of untold happiness and success to our youthful minds. " Delightful climate, glorious scenery, ideal place for the man with small capital, no income tax," and so on. . . .

There was also the letter John had received from his cousin Jim who had been " doing well out there " for several years. " A couple of thousand pounds or so," he wrote, " is all you need. Grow coffee, Kenya coffee is the finest in the world. Tea, too, is coming into its own ; anything grows in this place, it's a paradise, I tell you. Mind you," he went on, " I am not an expert as regards prices, but I am told that there is thirty pounds per acre clear profit to be made

out of coffee. Not bad, what ? " Cousin Jim was
the manager on a maize-plantation at a fixed salary ;
it was a job he got with influence. He was also an
optimist, a happy charming youth.

It was a clear day in October when our steamer
gently drifted out to sea. An icy breeze blew from
the shores of Southampton. Silent friends stood
desolately on the landing-stage . . . growing smaller
and smaller. No one had seen us off. John, turning
his back to the land and looking out to sea, held my
hand. It suddenly seemed ridiculous to me that a
small advertisement which he had picked up somewhere, and cousin Jim's letter (Jim, the optimistic
rascal of the family !) should thus have influenced
our lives ! Faint good-byes came floating seawards,
from where the afternoon sunlight was playing upon
the masts and the distant houses on the hill-tops were
gently silhouetted against the sky. Slowly England
faded into the mist, but no one seemed to feel depressed
for very long except, perhaps, a few middle-aged
women who looked as though they had left someone
behind ; a child or two, in all probability.

We travelled second-class and our part of the boat
was full of missionaries and returning farmers.
Anglican parsons hobnobbed with Non-Conformists,
and the more picturesque Capucins, French " white
fathers," Dominics, Mill Hill and priests, emaciated
Irish priests were returning again after a spell at
home, to their third or fourth bout of blackwater
fever. A holy crowd, nearly a hundred mortal souls,
bent on the salvation of others—yet presently feeling
as sea-sick as the rest of us who were journeying hither
to follow those poetic mirages which so easily mislead
the young.

Soon the air became bitterly cold and almost everyone went below to dress for dinner. A company of

elderly farmers gathered in the bar, other younger men walked restlessly in and out from deck to smoke-room with that air of men who have weeks of idleness ahead of them and wonder how to fill their time. . . . John and I sat in a quiet corner just over the engine, and our minds once again went back to the past. . . . Once more, perhaps, we wanted to convince ourselves that we had done well and acted wisely. As we sat there it seemed almost unbelievable that it was but yesterday that he and I had sat opposite each other in the tiny Mannington dining-room, whose only window faced a brick wall.

The bricks, I had noticed, were getting porous with the damp ; a bird had burst into song on the sooty little plum tree in the back garden ; a scraggy rhododendron, which had not bloomed for years, fought for its very existence in the patch of soil sur-rounded by asphalt. It was as though I had taken a photograph of every detail, to be remembered for ever.

For the last time I had stood by our bedroom window just as the sun was setting, the only place which had a certain amount of outlook. Some work-men were applying stucco to the house opposite, where lived the bright young thing whose husband went off to business in a yellow racing-car. The vicar's wife next door, who had once lived out in China, had brushed her lovely long hair in front of the mirror, which in common with all the mirrors in the avenue exposed its shabby back to the outside world. There was a plot of building-land to the right on which reposed a broken baby's cot, some rusty buckets, and in the way of a new addition, the scrapings of wall-paper of an entire house. The grace-ful lime tree in the minute front garden was rapidly losing its leaves ; the wind tore at the ivy which clung feebly to the stucco.

9

As I stood there, I tried to visualise the far-off tropics. How different, I dreamt, from this unfriendly manufacturing town ! What prisons people built for themselves ; how they worried to keep their walls around them ! Did not mankind spring from the wilds of the earth, and did it not subconsciously yearn to go back—somewhere where it was different, to a place like Kenya, for instance ? . . .

It was getting dark and the electric sign, advertising babies' food, was flashing its message in the distance. To me, barely conscious as a rule of its eternal pulse, the traffic had sounded like the distant drums of some African village. Africa obsessed me. I wanted freedom ; I wanted the sun. Winter, I shuddered, would soon be here again ; fog and dreary afternoons, church bazaars, windswept streets and smoking chimneys were rapidly approaching.

It was but yesterday that I had once more (and for the last time) gone to meet John at his father's shop, a draper's shop, where everything was " something— 11½d." Linoleum, stair-carpet, flannelette and art silk all at *x* 11½d. per yard. For the last time I had walked down the avenue, a short stretch of wooded corporation property, disturbing homeless couples defying the rain. Taking a short cut, I went through a dark passage which led past an old disused Jewish cemetery. Some nondescript middle-aged people climbed up the rickety staircase of an old house to a spiritualistic meeting. Poor souls, I thought, they ought to get away like John and me, then they would have less need to think of a future, better world. Further down the street I passed a Conservative club—*the* Conservative club of Mannington—its windows lit up, exposing a surprising amount of bald heads, belonging to a more solid world. I felt sorry even for the owners of the heads ! What a life, I sighed in a luxury of pity for half the world, cooped up and growing old, without ever having tasted freedom.

John had been delivering some bed-clothes to a county asylum, driving his father's old Ford through the poorest outskirts of the town, dodging children, inhaling fumes. Hundreds of dreary little houses, all alike, flew by reflected in the mirror of the car. . . . He was thinking of his great-grandfather, who had been a village blacksmith. *That* had been a man's job !

This was the last time he was going to deliver blankets at cut-throat prices. Yes, he was going to lead a man's life in future, in God's own country ; no more smoke, no more slums, no more haberdashery ; and above all, he was going to be his own boss. His rebellion had grown—and then given away again to commonsense, again and yet again. His mother though, who was a simple soul, had not long ago said to him : " Why not, my boy, face the problems at home, while there is still a chance ? " But now, youth had won the upper hand—once and for all.

# II

J OHN BEING RATHER DIFFIDENT, WE KEPT TO OUR-
selves on our voyage out. Besides, we did not want
to be obliged to spend our money by playing stupid
gambling games, buying drinks or joining expensive
excursions. A fair sprinkling of Government officials
travelled first class ; a few other, hopeful ones,
crowded together in the third. I met a stewardess
outside my cabin door and gave her ten shillings.
" Tip the stewardess beforehand," John's mother had
said, " and then she will do her best for you." A
steward, however, came and brought us all we
wanted, prepared our baths and attended me
when I was sick. I never saw the stewardess
again. . . .

In the meantime, all the younger crowd—especially
those who were returning after a holiday at home—
abandoned themselves to the most riotous fun.
They besieged the bar, they danced and flirted and
spent their money freely. The priests sat by themselves ; remote, sunk in meditation. But the parsons
and their self-assured wives were bent on making
friends. Knitting-needles rattled merrily amongst the
elderly. Two lady missionaries nearby sat comparing
notes on their comparative success. " I thought
Odero was saved," the younger one was saying, " he
seemed so changed ; he didn't any more—you know
what I mean—but as soon as I turned my back, the
devil tempted him again. He's been leading a wicked

life lately, and now," she sighed, " I have to save him all over again."

The ship's engineer winked at me as he went to the bar to have a drink with Rosey, the flirt of the ship. Rosey was young and unfashionably fat ; but because of her youth and ready tongue she possessed a certain voluptuous attraction. Slim girls paled before Rosey ; other women looked insipid. Rosey's cheeks were pink, her eyes danced, she sang the latest tunes, she played the piano and burst the camp-chairs. I surprised her in every hidden corner —first, second or third class, it was all the same to her—doling out caresses with ample generosity. She even made an attempt at being " *une femme sérieuse* " with one or two of the more picturesque monks. They were polite, but as she said in the smoke-room, " they're dead but they won't lie down."

The conversation at table, which we shared with some elderly people returning to Kenya, opened out a new world to me. New threatening possibilities were to be in store for us in our future Eden. Remarks made casually will remain locked in my memory for ever. . . . Malaria, smallpox, blights, pests, droughts, floods, cattle diseases, East-Coast fever, rinderpest and politics were the main topics of con- versation. Almost with an intuitive clairvoyance, I saw John's future in this strange land, and for a little while I grew afraid. Not for myself, but for him. It was his battle, his hopes, his future ; it would be his Hell—and so become mine, too. I hoped too, that unlike some of these men, he would know when he was licked before it was too late.

They were not, as a whole, a sensitive crowd. If they had been and their hardships which they discussed so freely were true (and they were poor into the bargain), they could hardly have been conscious of their true conditions. They were mostly much older than John, and had lost that fire which still smouldered in his eyes. Some appeared brutalised, drawing their romance from the whisky bottle. Perhaps, too, like farmers all the world over, they liked grousing.

"It's a man's life, my dear young lady," said one of them to me one evening. "There's not much you can do, you know, except look after your man."

"He'll need some looking after, that fellow, by the looks of him. Don't let him work too hard. Remember you are on the Equator."

An actress, the most popular woman after Rosey, left the boat at Suez. She was a jolly blonde, immensely self-reliant. "Too-d'l-loo," she called from the quay, generously throwing kisses. The ship's engineer waved to her until she was out of sight.

Our cabin was next door to a six-berth men's cabin in which were two farmers and four cadaverous priests. These French priests used to rise according to habit, I expect, about 4.30 a.m.—long before the decks were swept. Breviaries in hand, they walked by themselves in unworldly silence.

"These fellows never seem to have a bath." I recognised the voice of the farmer I had spoken to.

I could hear every word these men said, as there was a ventilator leading from their inside cabin to our outside one. John being a good sleeper, however, was not so easily disturbed.

"If only they washed their feet," said another, "I shouldn't mind."

"Queer crowd, anyway," replied the first.

"A little mad, poor devils."

"Aye," said the other, a Lincolnshire cattle dealer. "It's a mad world. . . . That couple next to our table, they're going out to make their fortune. . . ."

14

" Aye, there's something to be said for them, but,"
he yawned, " I'm mighty glad I've got my youth
behind me."

" Someone ought to warn them, though."

" No use, let them find out by themselves. Have
they any money? "

" A couple of thousand pounds or so, so the young
woman said."

They both laughed.

" Might sell them that dud bit at the far-end of
my place ; rocks, bushes and no water."

" Farming," said the cattle-dealer, " is a dud's game
anyway. Why don't you tell the girl to start a hat-
shop or a beauty parlour . . . damned sight better
than cultivating virgin ground."

Again they laughed, uproariously this time. I
hated them. They seemed coarse and callous, and
I resolutely refused to believe a word they said. After
all, what was to stop us from making good if we
really wanted to ?

## III

SLOWLY WE SAILED INTO THE SHELTERED HARBOUR, a coral island of one's childhood dreams. Below it was almost like a stage set for a pantomime. A cheerful noisy pandemonium, pale clusters of palms, porters shouting and the ship's band playing a boisterous march. One had arrived for good or evil, so help us God. We wanted to sing for joy, glad to be there at last ; glad to have escaped from the atrophy of Mannington. Why hadn't we come before to create, to build a new world for ourselves ? We both thought of our industrial home-town in the north ; cold, grey and chilly. What a contrast ! Yes, we were going to like it—weren't we ? Some more whiskies and sodas, stewards being tipped, Rosey waving frantically to someone on shore.

An Anglican clergyman whose service I had once attended came to say good-bye. He shook my hand and gave me his blessing.

" My dear," he said, " never let your enthusiasm die ! "

" Of course not," I laughed at the fussy old chap. I am afraid I was not interested in the blessings of the middle-aged. Mercifully the young ones do not know when the old ones are sorry for them.

There amongst the crowd stood cousin Jim, clad in very abbreviated shorts and a khaki shirt which exposed a very hairy chest. Cousin Jim grown very thin.

" Well, old sport," he patted John on the back.
" I am glad you have taken the plunge ! "

Some extremely tall and smart native policemen
stood at attention by the landing-stage. Some
fetching negresses, most picturesquely clad in gaudy
wraps, hovered in the background. It struck me
that however casual the English may be about
appearances, especially in the case of some of their
buildings, they could never be accused of slovenliness
in matters military. The native bobbies looked
splendid in their khaki shorts, tunics and red sashes.

" See you later, old sport," cousin Jim called out
to an anxious-looking, equally thin young man who
stood expectantly amongst the waiting crowd.

" That's Marsden, one of my friends," said Jim,
" he is getting married this afternoon, and I am to
be best man. His fiancée was on your boat . . .
he hasn't seen her for five solid years . . . hardly
remembers her. He's feeling a bit shaky, old
Marsden. I reckon there is many a fellow who's
married a stranger at this Cathedral, worse luck."

" Not a bad place, is it ? " Jim went on amongst
the din, while John attended to the customs. " All
you want to do, Joan, is not to take anything seriously
in this country. Anything might happen, you know
. . . alive to-day and dead to-morrow."

Equipped with that amount of philosophy, I realised
we might as well have carried on at home.

" Oh, by the way, Joan, do you still play the
organ ? Good girl, I want you to play for Marsden
at two-thirty this afternoon. The train won't leave
till five-thirty. Probably there'll be no room on it,
anyway . . . depends if the porter gets you a place.
Besides, let's celebrate to-night at the hotel."

" As a matter of fact, Jim," I replied, " we have
very little money, and every pound we spend

B                    17

unnecessarily is a pound wasted." Cousin Jim appeared to be surprised. He looked at me and then he laughed.

"Good old Mannington," he roared. . . . "Sorry," he apologised, a moment later, " but it's priceless ! You see, no one minds the pounds in this country. If they did they might as well be dead."

John, having seen to the immigration formalities and the luggage, wanted to have a look at the island.

" Righto," said Jim, " but for God's sake let's go and have a drink first."

We went to Jim's hotel, a surprisingly up-to-date place. The bar was filling rapidly. It was easy to recognise the old-timers from the new-comers. Manners and clothes were different ; the new-comers were much more conventional in both. It was the old-timers who did all the talking, and it was they who eventually got drunk.

" Christ ! " murmured Jim, " I wish I could make Marsden drunk . . . got engaged before he left . . . came out to make a home for his girl. Took him five years . . . a one-roomed house with a partition in the middle."

Jim was quite unaware, as usual, of the grim humour of his reminiscences. A not-so-young fellow stood talking quietly to a serious young man dressed entirely in white, also a new-comer. He wore a beard and a bright blue shirt.

" As long as I stop here I am all right," he said, " but as soon as I set my foot in Europe, I am laid low again. Marvellous place this for T.B. ; but as for this so-called lure of Africa, my dear chap, it's about as empty as death."

" Good Lord," answered the other, " how perfectly ghastly. Whatever do you do with yourself ? "

" Counting sheep mostly, and sending them through the dip for my aunt up on the Kidwang estate."

They, too, were both a little drunk.

" As for the women," the one with the beard went on, " they are just like cows. There comes a time when you fairly long for a white woman, someone you can talk to, you know."

A very young-looking old-timer, aggressively drunk, was telling the crowd by the cocktail-bar that there were at the moment three women in love with him in this blessed island. One of them a Greek, married of course, but that did not matter. He'd thrown her husband out of the window only the other day. The blighter had begun to interfere.

" Oh, shut up ! " shouted Jim as he hastily emptied his glass.

I finished my cocktail and went upstairs to wash my hands. Two white women walked in front of me, dressed in riding breeches and topees.

" What can you expect," one of them was saying with the utmost contempt, " she comes from Mannington."

My home town was being labelled " not so nice." I resented it. Quite unaccountably I was losing my temper. In what way could Mannington have sinned, I wondered, that these exiles or colonials should thus pass judgment ? Moved as we had been by romantic longings to leave this midland town, I now wanted passionately to defend it. I did not, in the face of Mombasa's almost unendurable heat, remember its dreariness. Living at about ninety degrees in the shade, one abruptly ceased to be critical of any other place.

John and I went to have one more look at our boat which had housed us so well for nearly a month. A trading-ship was leaving to battle against the

Indian Ocean. Two natives on the grimy deck turned to the east, asking for the blessings of Allah. Two intensely haughty-looking camels stood outside an antique- and curio-shop, peeping into the upstairs window. The town was a medley of trolley cars, ox-wagons, Arabs, Somalis in robes, white men in shorts and pith helmets, natives in smart clothes, natives practically naked, some proud-looking, others servile. Smart white women, dowdy white women ; and above all the hot, glaring sun. It seemed a cheerful place, everyone talked and chatted, especially the negroes, who walked noiselessly, like shadows. . . .

We all met at the Cathedral punctually at 2.30. Cousin Jim was wearing some slightly better clothes. A negro took me to the organ-loft, where I sat by the keyboard, ready to play at the signal from the local vicar. It was a gloomy place, but it seemed to cheer up when Marsden walked in with none other than Rosey on his arm ! Rosey dressed in pink ; her roguish radiance was priceless to behold. Good old Rosey. Conscious of the sacred purpose of the moment, Marsden stood by the altar utterly bewildered. " It will bring on his malaria," whispered Jim, in an audible whisper, " any excitement does." When the ceremony was over, and I had played the Wedding March, the five of us went back to the hotel and had a bottle of champagne. Marsden felt somewhat shy of his bonny bride ; the Rosey of his dreams, yet so much more self-assured, so much more rotund than she had been five years ago.

" Now I am here to look after you," she said, looking him up and down, " I'll see to it that you get a bit fatter. Skin and bone, that's what you are, both of you " ; her eyes including cousin Jim. The real Rosey, I decided, as I ventured forth into the bazaar to buy her an Indian wedding-present, would make him a good wife.

We changed our clothes in Jim's bedroom, which contained an enormous brass double-bed which was shrouded in a canopy of mosquito-netting. We donned our brand-new khaki clothes, which we were told to buy at home. " Everyone wears khaki in Kenya," they said. Khaki did not suit me, nor did it, I noticed, suit anyone else. Women did not, I found, wear it as a rule ; and those who did apparently did not mind the livery hue which it imparted to their complexions. We said good-bye to Marsden and his wife, who sat on the hotel verandah looking rather lonely, wondering what to do for the rest of the day. There was, in fact, nothing to do except explore the little island, which was soon done ; or to go for a swim which from all accounts might be very pleasant. Rosey seemed to me, for the first time since I had set eyes upon her, to be at a loose end. It looked as though she and her newly acquired husband would have to get to know each other all over again.

# IV

W E MANAGED TO SECURE OUR PLACES ON THE train shortly after the wedding, leaving cousin Jim behind to celebrate. John hated wasting time. The carriages were hopelessly crowded, as they always were after the arrival of a boat. Natives, too, seemed to have taken to travelling by train, and often spent their savings on a lengthy railway journey, just for the fun of it. Some were almost naked, others were clad in half-crown khaki shorts, all of them happily as yet without class-distinction, crowding into a couple of carriages behind the engine. . . . A seething mass of black limbs, all apparently alike, flashing teeth and raucous voices. Up hill it went, the little wood-fed engine ; pulling for all it was worth, slowly at first, then excitedly, puffing and panting like a fussy old lady trying to catch a tram.

At the outset it was a fascinating trip ; the sea on both sides of us ; a few islands, then the mainland sprinkled with palms, acacias and native huts. There were frequent stops at stations, which were at first interesting enough, but which grew monotonous as the journey proceeded. Dozens of black beauties stood watching the train, chewing sugar-cane, divinely indifferent to the world around. Young women with budding figures, old women with dried-up flesh ; all of them with the calm expression of meditating cows.

" Hi, *bibi* (woman)," drunkenly called a White

man from one of the carriages, "*cuja hapa* (come here)."

They took no notice of him. With perfect *sang-froid anglais*, they eyed him coolly with their calm brown eyes, until the youngest of them burst out into a sudden harsh giggle, for all the world like a factory girl.

The land we were passing through looked fertile enough—if one could judge it by the amazing profusion of bushes and scrub. For miles we passed through a disused sisal plantation, a mere wilderness of some company's forlorn hope. Several Americans who had also been swallowed up on our boat, first class though, were in the carriage immediately behind us. " Say, King Kong," one of them called out to a fine-looking native, during one of the lengthy stops at a tin-shanty railway station, " come here." The negro approached rather hesitantly, as if he might get a biff on the head if he ventured too close. " What's your name ? " he called. The negro shook his head ; he had not understood : " Me Swahili," he answered.

" Swahili ? He's a Swahili ? " the American shouted back into the carriage.

" Ask him to sing," said someone, a woman. " Tell him he's a fine-looking guy, I like him," another female voice called out. " George, where's that Swahili grammar ? "

" *Mezuri sana*, Swahili," said the girl from the carriage-window, holding the book in her hand. The negro bowed slightly, saluted stiffly and then walked away superbly indifferent.

" Oh, boy, but isn't he just cute ! " the girl screamed.

This Swahili, I felt, was worthy of the British Empire.

At sunset we arrived at another tin-shanty station

where we were served a fairly decent supper by a Greek. It was mutton. I was to get to know mutton well in the days to come ! The station dining-room was crowded and we were served in relays whilst the train was refuelled with blocks of wood. Apparently the same Indian station-master, as at all the previous stations, was eventually stopped by one of the Americans.

" Here, Tarzan," he said, holding him by his flowing clothes which partly exposed the most untarzanlike hairy, bowed legs. " What's the big idea ? " he asked when the official stopped salaaming. " What's the big idea of letting all these duskies drive in the front carriages, so that we, who are leewards, get all their unholy smells ? This travelling hole-of-Calcutta has completely upset my stomach."

" Sorry, sir," said the Indian, salaaming again profusely.

" Don't do that," cried the American, " go and get something done about it."

A signal was given and off we went again into the silence of the night, the engine belching glowing cinders over the train, like falling stars. For half the night the Americans sat on the carriage steps talking. Round about midnight I rose from my couch and beheld another little station in complete darkness, except for a hurricane lamp.

" Excuse me, Madam," said the American who had gone for a stroll clad in striped pyjamas, " have you by any chance any insecticide with you ? We find it quite impossible to sleep ; it's those nigger trucks in front ; they should be at the back."

I immediately began to itch—such is the power of suggestion. I had some Keating's powder somewhere at the bottom of the trunk, but in the darkness I handed him some talcum-powder by mistake.

At dawn, after a fitful sleep, I was awakened by a rifle-shot. Peeping out of the window I saw what seemed to me to be hundreds of human heads—white heads, brown heads and black heads—wagging in violent discussion. Looking out upon a barren plain I could see a couple of giraffes feeding off the uppermost twigs of a dry-looking mimosa tree, whilst two ostriches lollopped into the distance and a small gazelle was running for its very life. Everyone wondered who fired the shot. I strongly suspected one of the Americans, who were the only passengers apparently fast asleep. Looking into the mirror, I found my face, hair, clothes—in fact the whole carriage—covered with a thick layer of red dust. The whole landscape was tinged with this unreal colour, the nearby hillocks and the distant hills were of copper-coloured earth which made them look artificial in the blazing morning sun. A wilderness of red dust lay everywhere.

After a faint glimpse of mount Kilimanjaro which towered above the mist, we had breakfast of bacon and eggs at another tiny railway station. Presently the American returned my talcum-powder. " I reckon we'll have to get kind of used to vermin, now we are here," he said.

" Good morning, sir," he called out to the engine-driver, who was a White man. " How do?" and offered him a fat cigar.

Tired and unwashed, we set off again into the heat of another day.

# V

WITH ITS NEWNESS, I THOUGHT NAIROBI WOULD please the Americans. Some very fine buildings alternated with the most miserable makeshift bungalows. Bedraggled pepper trees and pale sweet-smelling eucalyptus trees were vainly trying to shade the main road. Armies of cars of every age and description, as well as a few rickshaws, seemed to be dodging weary oxen ; and native women fantastically loaded, mostly with an infant slung like a knapsack over their shoulders as well as a load of wood about their own weight, crowded the thoroughfare. Docile, ox-eyed, the women walked along in the dust, barefoot and contented ; their lords and masters swaggering ahead, carrying spears.

Having booked a room by wire in Jim's favourite hotel, which was surprisingly modern, we were spared the trouble our acquaintances had, who found all the hotels full. Everyone we noticed had brought their own servants, who slept out in a native hotel They cleaned one's shoes and saw to every other need, except of course one's food ; thus one's life became immediately more complicated and much more expensive. However, we decided to do without a " boy."

The very first thing we did was to have a hot bath. The plumbing we found to our joy was up to date and the water really hot. Luckily I was quite used to getting my own bath ready. Baths over, we then had a meal—mutton again, and very tough. Indeed, we were soon to learn that it was mutton nearly every day and invariably tough !

We did not at first go out with the idea of sight-seeing, but to visit all the land agents in the town. John hated losing time ; time, to us, was money. It was market-day in Nairobi or so it seemed to us. Later we found out that it was always market-day ! The natives, we noticed, were anything but down-hearted ; British rule did not apparently oppress them. They sang, shouted and argued and were told to shut up by a black policeman, as they were disturbing the proceedings within the shabby court-house. Thoroughly fascinated by the motley crowd, dodging cars driven by grotesquely-dressed chauffeurs, I waited for John, who presently returned looking somewhat sobered. His visit to the agents had produced few results. There were plenty of farms for sale and any amount of land, but the price was usually beyond our means, or else the places were a hundred and fifty miles or so from the nearest railway station.

The last agent we called on sat in his office with his feet up on the window-sill, his double felt hat pushed back, exposing a livery countenance. He was reading a novel, *The Boathouse Murder*. His bare forearms, which should have been bandaged, were covered with sun sores. Presently he asked us what we wanted after he carefully closed his book. He did not seem to think much of us somehow.

" Hi, *toto*," he called out into the street, where several negroes squatted on their heels, " hand me those files quickly."

The *toto* (youth) quick as lightning reached for a bundle of very dusty papers, which his boss could easily have reached himself had he taken his feet off the window-sill. In any case, it was not a very

comfortable position to do business in. The fountain-
pen was dry and the agent swore. " Its farming you
want to go in for ? " he asked, collecting his legs at
last. John explained what he was prepared to pay,
and declined, for obvious reasons, the offer of several
five to ten thousand acre farms.

" There is not much on my books," the fellow said,
" at least, not at your price. It *is* farming you want
to go in for ? " he asked once more, as though he
thought we might be tempted to try something else—
considering the scarcity of small farms. " Ah, well,"
he sighed, handing John a couple of addresses, " I
wish you luck."

" Thanks. Could you, by any chance, suggest
anything better ? " John, already on the defensive,
asked. I don't know why he asked ; for nothing as
far as I could see would change John's mind for him
now.

" Could I suggest anything better ? Indeed, sir, I
think I could ; but it's not exactly my business. For
one thing, I have still got to come across the man who
has made any money in this country by farming alone,
or any other kind of hard work. I farmed once," he
went on, " and now I've got this job." He yawned,
and then sat down again.

" Well, I'm going to try anyway," said John.
" After all, it's making a living I'm after in the first
instance."

" Oh, well, no one's yet starved in this
country ; barring niggers, of course, during regular
droughts. . . .

John then went to buy a tent and some cooking-
pots. " There's no sense in spending money on hotel
bills, is there ? " he asked.

The following day Jim arrived with Marsden and
Rosey. Marsden had a touch of fever and looked

slightly dazed with quinine. Rosey, still radiant and dressed in white linen, went out shopping on her own. During dinner the crowd at the hotel grew very hilarious. Ladies and gentlemen, drunkenly cheerful, were upholding the prestige of the Empire in evening dress. Jim looked depressed ; he looked as though he had slightly coarsened. He had had several drinks already. Presently we were joined by other young men who also had had numerous drinks, which somewhat belied their insistence that it was a happy life that they were leading, and that " by jove, they would not live at home again, not if you paid them." We were treated to cocktails and had to treat again in turn. I sighed within over so much useless expenditure. Feeling rather worried after our visit to the land agent, I asked Jim about these periodical droughts that I had been told of. " Lord," said Jim, " it's all in the game. We've only had two since I've been here ; besides, you get them at home, don't you ? " Rosey, now dressed in red and looking very hot indeed, nudged Marsden to come to bed. " Silly," she said, " boozing like that."

John and I went upstairs to sit on the verandah. An Indian snake-charmer who had been begging by the entrance to the hotel was wrapping up his paraphernalia. . . . Giant bull-frogs croaked in the prominent gutters of Nairobi. " I shall have to leave you by yourself rather a lot these next few weeks," said John suddenly. " We must try to get a home together as soon as we can, and then we'll show the old folks at home that we can achieve something as well as they."

John had three letters of introduction which friends of the family who had someone " out in Africa who was doing well " had given him. One of them, whom John visited a few hours further up country, was just

trying to sell out after a struggle of seven years'
duration. John returned that night, slightly dashed
in spirits. Another friend of the family lived about
thirty miles outside the town, a mere stone's throw
according to local ideas. Someone, a friend of Jim's,
lent John a horse which he rode there and back again
the following day. Never having ridden before, he
returned too sore either to sit or speak. His clothes
were riddled with ticks, an objectionable bug which
clings to the grass but feeds on animal blood, thus
carrying and spreading disease. The letter of introduction had brought John to a youngish man, who
promptly tried to sell his farm.

When John disclosed the actual size of our capital,
this friend of the folks at home plainly lost all interest
in us. The third letter was to a fellow who lived
in Rhodesia—several thousand miles away. Kenya,
Tanganyika, Rhodesia and South Africa—it's all the
same to the folks at home ! John took his tent and
went on " safari," that is, to trek about the country.
He took with him a native-carrier who was to cook
and wash for him. He was away for weeks sometimes.
One day he wrote that he had at last been offered a
farm at £1 per acre, not too far from the railway
(about 45 miles, that was all) ; but upon closer
investigation he found that there was no water. . . .
The owner, however, was an ingenious fellow, irritable
and peevish though he might be. Blessed with several
steam-jets which continuously belched forth from his
volcanic ground, the farmer fastened a piece of iron
sheeting above one of these fountains of steam and
thus collected his minute water-supply—literally drop
by drop—as it splashed from the iron sheet into a bath
tub. This unique and so far constant water-supply
did not, however, justify the price he was asking for the
place, which was known in the district as " Distilled

Water." It was the kind of farm, John wrote, that young fellows were known to have bought without ever having seen them.

At last the first batch of letters arrived from England. . . . They hinted that we were expected to show some signs of success before long, and that " having made our beds we were also expected to lie on them."

After this splendid piece of encouragement, we decided that Kenya had at least the advantage of being a long way from home.

It was now rapidly nearing Christmas, and still there was no money coming in. Having taken a cheap room at the back of the hotel, facing a rubbish-heap, and refusing several opportunities to " enjoy myself while I was yet young," I began to think of ways and means of doing some work myself. A charming old gentleman-farmer from up country told me that John would find it very difficult to obtain a farm at his own price. If he did, it would probably be some distance from the railway, and so make delivery difficult and expensive. He also said (which was common knowledge) that it was impossible to get a job, that nothing very useful could be learned by listening to conflicting advice and that the conditions of soil and the rainfall sometimes varied every three miles, or less, and that every farmer had to experiment entirely on his own. A great deal of money, alas, was lost on making mistakes.

" This is not a reliable country, and it has not a reliable normal rainfall. It might be better," the old man went on, " from a purely financial point of view, if your young husband did something else with his money. There are shop-keepers who have grown rich."

When I told John of this interview, he merely

31

replied : " But hang it all, Joan, what have I come here for, except to farm ? "

Shortly after Christmas I saw an advertisement in the local paper which aroused my interest. . . . A lady wanted a companion to assist her in a boarding house. I went to see her at once. Her spacious wooden bungalow was situated in one of Nairobi's suburbs known as " The Hill." The lady's husband, a Government official, had gone away for several months, and being bored with her own company she decided to try to make a bit of money. She had a very good cook, an enormous Kavirondo, well over six feet tall and very broad into the bargain. " He'll make a fine chucker-out in case of emergency," the young lady observed.

We came to some agreement about sharing the work and responsibilities as well as the profits—which considering that the house, furniture and the risk was hers—showed a great spirit of generosity on her part. Yet this woman had a most amazing streak of meanness, and her pet economy was the richshaw boys, who never got their due. Now my partner was a heavy woman, and it was no joke to pull her up the steep hill to her home. She usually paid the boys in small coins which took them a very long time to count. Long after she was back home again, the boys would still be sitting outside counting their money. Sometimes a passer-by would count the coins for them. When the natives were thoroughly convinced that they had not received their proper fare, plus tips, they came' up to the house and rang the bell. There usually followed a lengthy rigmarole.

" All right," my friend said, " give me that money back."

The boys innocently handed her the money, whereupon she slammed the door in their faces.

" That will teach them a lesson ! " she said. If
they rang the bell again, which usually happened, the
chucker-out was fetched from the kitchen. This
gigantic living threat finished the argument with a
single look ! Next day a native policeman, probably
a friend or a brother of the rickshaw fellow, came to
the door, demanding that the boys be paid. My
friend then handed the money to him, which was
again counted at leisure—and found to be short.
Again she called the chucker-out and the policeman
withdrew. Really, it was as good as keeping a dog !
By the end of the month there was not a rickshaw boy
in the whole of Nairobi who did not know the *memsahib* on the hill, the *memsahib* with the *m'pishi*
(cook).

At the end of two months there was not a thing
we did not know about lodgers. We had housed
about a dozen minor Government officials, some female
secretaries, a couple of commercial travellers and a
wine merchant. The walls of the house were thin,
mere wooden partitions, and if not actually seen they
could be heard. There never was sufficient bath
water. It had to be carried, bucket by bucket, and
poured into a most joyless galvanised iron-tub. . . .

The women guests had an amazing capacity for
drinking tea, and brewed it in their rooms at all hours
of the day and night. The plot of grass at the back of
the house was covered with tea-leaves. And when they
were not brewing tea, they were ironing their clothes.
Their conversation was equally unenterprising. One of
the officials, a weedy young man from some obscure
home in London, had the habit of putting his feet on
the dining-room table. Perhaps it was the lack of a
mantelpiece or the habit of a lifetime, or again perhaps
it was his way of showing that he felt at home. My
colonial partner said nothing until one evening she

fetched the chucker-out, tipped him two shillings and said : " Omera, you can throw him out the very next time he puts his feet on the table." The negro grinned. It was enough. Our boarder left next day.

At church on Sunday the cook knelt in a pew in front of me, wearing one of my silk nightdresses round his neck as a scarf. He had borrowed it from the laundry-basket.

It was just after the wine merchant had had an attack of delirium tremens, which almost shook the flimsy bungalow, that to my great relief John returned to fetch me. He had at last been able to find a plot of land of a thousand acres which cost exactly a thousand pounds. It was situated in some valley up country, thirty miles from the nearest station.

# VI

I WAS GLAD TO LEAVE NAIROBI. LOOKING BACK, THE impressions which remain most vividly in my mind are an expanse of bungalows in the beautiful wooded outskirts ; a dusty, parched newness within the town, a hectic restless coming and going. . . . I remember faces, some fanatical, belonging to Somalis and Arabs ; bovine faces belonging to natives ; worried faces ; sick faces ; bored faces and faces (belonging to the White races) downright sad or alcoholic. Nairobi took the sheen out of my enthusiasm. It took it out of others, too. Occasionally I used to meet an old face I had met on the boat ; slightly dashed, finding things very expensive, capital available grossly inadequate.

The only perfectly contented faces I remember were those of the Indians and Goanese. To them Nairobi must have seemed like home. Even that bunch of dirty rags which arrived punctually at 9 a.m. at the boarding-house on the hill, to empty the slops, salaaming profusely ; yes, even this " untouchable " who did the jobs the natives would not do, looked happy. He, too, had his place in the sun, more so perhaps. Unlike the White man, he did not expect too much. I also remember the Indian bazaar, where Indian shopkeepers manufactured shirts for the natives and rattled their Singer sewing-machines out of doors, letting the snippings fall into the street to mingle with the refuse of every other trade which was plied in their neighbourhood. . . . Barbers cut the long hair of their customers by holding their heads between their knees. Snip, snip, snip. The lank black hair of an Indian customer fell to the ground as he knelt in front of the barber.

It was March when we left Nairobi, and it was raining. It never rained for long—a couple of hours or so and then the sky was clear again. We were told that the rains were not so good this season. From the train we had a view of some magnificent coffee plantations, of natives sitting on the cultivator seats, combing the red earth. For some time we travelled through the most fertile districts of Kenya, and it struck me forcibly what an enormous amount of labour and capital have been spent in Kenya by private individuals. The journey also reminded me of my school-days, which I spent abroad, in a school where there were German, French and Italian girls. The teacher, knowing no better, told us the legend of how England drew enormous riches from her colonies. I expect these French, German and Italian girls still believe it, and so will their children after them. . . .

It was about midnight when we arrived at Nymba. John had sent a wire to the one and only hotel of the place, but there was no one to meet us. There was practically no light anywhere. Someone said the hotel was just down the road. John and I, hanging on to each other, staggered out into the dark, making a bee-line for the only house which was faintly lit up. Bumping into trees, narrowly escaping dykes, getting entangled with wire-netting, we eventually found ourselves on a verandah. Within, all by himself, his feet on the desk, a bottle of whisky at his side and reading by the flickering light of home-made electricity, sat a pale, tired-looking man of middle age. John knocked gently at the door, loath to disturb him. Slowly the man rose and opened the grill. Peering out into the dark passage and espying us, he seemed greatly surprised. Our wire had not arrived, he had not expected anyone. It would probably arrive to-morrow. . . .

"Ah well, there might and there might not be a room for you."

Cautiously the man opened doors here and there, all the way down the passage. He could never be sure, he said, if the room was taken, as some people just walked in and didn't bother to tell him until next morning. None of the occupants seemed to bother about locking their doors. The rooms were all alike, smelling strongly of disinfectant ; two single beds stood in each, clean but very primitive. Twice the manager disturbed a sleeping guest and was told to " hop it." Our room, at the end of the passage, had recently been whitewashed and reminded me strongly of a hospital. A dressing-table completely blocked the window, and the linoleum had been patched with numerous different coloured pieces of material. The " untouchable " had left a generous supply of Jeyes' fluid in every conceivable place. There was no wardrobe, no chest of drawers. In a country of shorts and khaki shirts, a couple of nails behind the door did just as well. " Don't put your shoes outside," the manager said, as he too went away to bed, yawning pitifully.

Neither of us slept until nearly dawn. There was no air ; an electric dynamo throbbed somewhere in the distance, dogs barked and beds creaked. We lay in the dark and contemplated, and grew increasingly depressed. Asleep at last, we were promptly awakened by a native who brought us pale and lukewarm cups of tea. Before I was up, " the bundle of clothes " arrived, salaaming three times and politely leaving his sandals outside the door. The fellow had to start early in order to finish his round, as he was the only scavenger in Nymba.

Presently I discovered a bathroom with a small galvanised iron bath which required to be filled by bucket, and emptied again by the same process. No one, we found, ever used it. I, too, decided to do without. We were given a very nice breakfast, though, in a spacious dining-room where there were mostly men feeding : old-timers everyone of them, discussing the weather, the crops and their cattle.

A white woman arrived in a gig with a very sick baby. The hotel, I found, was used as a hospital for White people, for there was nowhere else for them to go. A baby was born the very next night in a room near ours. I distinctly heard its plaintive cry as it arrived in this strange, mosquito-infested world. The local doctor and his wife were the only ones in attendance.

Curious, I went to view the little town. Alas, I was forced to view it for four weeks, for there was still much for John to do, buying implements for clearing bushes, a wagon, a plough, spades, harness and a mill to grind the maize for the natives' food. Nymba, a small administrative township, boasted two churches, a native hospital, an hotel, a bank, a garage with one Ford for hire, two clubs and a native bazaar—where White people bought their groceries and were sometimes heavily in debt to the Indian merchants. A third-rate little township, Nymba's scanty population, which gathered round the club bar or in the ladies' reading-room of an evening, was for the most part a rather forsaken community of exiles, boasting about six different class distinctions. One poor heroic woman I found was a class entirely for herself, being the wife of a small greengrocer. The men, I noticed, would probably have mixed ;

but the women, exiled though they were, remained pathetically middle-class, each trying to surpass the other. It was only the pioneer type of woman, the woman who knew how to rough it and had at one time or other grown conscious of her lonely plight, who rose above such things. She and only she gained a proper sense of values.

As in Nairobi, the bull-frogs croaked incessantly at the close of day ; there seemed an indescribable resignation not only in the silences but in the very sounds of the tropics. The fellows who gathered at the bar, I knew, would not have thought so ; they were making merry in a crude sort of way. One of them had sold some land, and was now generously treating everyone all round. Probably he had not spoken to a soul for a year or more, having lived somewhere in the bush. Finally, after several unsteady games of darts, he started aiming at the liqueur-bottles on the shelf, shooting them down one after the other with an automatic pistol. His aim was good and the precious fluid flowed stickily all over the shelves and on to the floor. The negro behind the bar, with perfect dignity and without a smile, picked up the fragments of glass and licked his fingers. I have often wondered what he thought. . . .

Every afternoon at tea-time White women gathered on the lawn of the club with their few children, talking like women all the world over about clothes, servants —harassed middle-class women, completely unchanged by environment, pathetically interested in the *Tatler*. Listening to their talk for several weeks on end, it seemed significant that they spoke mostly of Home. " When I was at home," " When I go home," " You can get it at Selfridges." They spoke of the latest London play as if they had seen it. Slowly, reluctantly, the conversation switched over

39

to local gossip ; a little spicy perhaps, but forgivable. " Did you know the Vet's wife was once a barmaid ? " " They say X's wife had been a waitress in a Lyons' Corner House."

One or two bright but not so young things, whose husbands farmed nearby, blew in, clad in shorts and open shirts, powdered knees and beauty spots cunningly applied on the chest ; genuine Mayfair, the kind who was evading Income Tax at home. I was beginning to know who was who amongst the hundred and one men who dropped in at the club or at the hotel. Most of them, the manager told me, had private means. It struck me that anyone reputed to be unusually enterprising or more than usually successful, either as an experimental farmer or as an ordinary shopkeeper, almost invariably turned out to be Scotch.

John, having bought a bicycle at the local garage, had gone down the Simba valley to our future home in order to set some men cutting bushes and preparing a coffee bed. Having taken a room in the annex for economy's sake, I remained at the hotel waiting for him to fetch me, as well as our goods and chattels. At one of Nymba's periodical sales I bought a cooking-stove, some beds, a table and some chairs, a sofa and a small sideboard, also a wardrobe. They were the effects of someone who had departed for good ; unsung and quickly forgotten. At this pathetic little sale even the dresses of a White woman were being sold against the debts left behind by a couple who had come to make their fortune, but had instead lost their money as well as their health. The dresses were bought by some native women, who slipped them on there and then, causing a great deal of laughter.

Many a half-hour I sat on the hotel verandah, getting stung by mosquitoes and contemplating the moon. . . . I gazed out over the majestic plain surrounding Nymba and felt oppressed by the weird silence which seemed to be brooding over the magnificent, yet puny, efforts of the little White man. Sometimes the manager joined me for a smoke. Bilious though he looked, he had that charming happy-go-lucky, devil-may-care attitude of the old-timer towards life.

" So you are off down the Simba valley ? " he asked.

I could sense by the way that he asked this perfectly ordinary question that he had not a very great opinion of the place.

" Do you know it ? " I questioned, hoping for some further information.

It seemed to me that I was getting far more information than John—information which was far from encouraging.

" There's that Simba lake at the bottom of your place, isn't there ? "

" A lake ? How lovely ! " This was the first that I had heard of it.

" Well," the manager went on, " some call it a lake, but it's only a swamp, really. . . . Plenty of mosquitoes though . . . best thing to do is to take a dose of quinine every night."

I was silent ; it touched me deeply that this man, whom people might call common at a glance, should have beneath his loud and cheery manner some understanding beyond that of any single woman in the whole of Nymba.

" Yes," he sighed to himself as he took another sip of whisky, " it's invariably the less cultured who stand it best. . . . Rough chaps like me."

" What about the land itself, is it any good ? Tell me the truth if you can," I asked him under cover of the darkness. He did not reply at once. Presently he said :

" I do not know ; no one has farmed there yet. It will be all experiment for you. It's the fellow who sold it to you who's made his pile. He bought half the valley, some twenty miles or so, ten years before the War. He bought it for a song. He did not farm it for there was no need. . . . Speculate, I say, if you can. You cannot work in this climate. Look at me," he added, " I tried it once. Pah," he kicked a stool away, " take no notice of what I say ! Let me get you a glass of port ; it will do you the world of good. Listen," he whispered as he handed me the glass, " if you want to buy a plot of land right in the centre of this township, I'll see that you get it cheap. That's what you want—buy where a town develops. Think it over . . . and to your health."

His advice was splendid, but I could not follow it, having no money of my own.

A couple of Fords came crunching on the gravel. Young men had brought two lady bank-clerks home from a jaunt. The girls were very plain and long past their youth, but they were the only spinsters in the whole of Nymba. The prison clock struck twelve when I roused myself from my dreams, and went to bed. I had in the spirit bought a township, discovered a gold-mine and gone to end my days in a cottage by the sea.

# VII

I HAD BEEN FEELING FAIRLY SEEDY FOR SOME TIME.
I therefore decided to go and see the doctor before
I departed down the valley. The little native
hospital lay right on the outskirts of the town.
A handful of prisoners dreamily dug up the road
outside the gates ; the warder yawned and spat,
squatting under a pepper tree. One of the men, a
thief or murderer by all accounts, began to sing
cheerfully and the rest joined in—slowly, rhythmically.
From the adjoining field a rabbit scurried across the
road. With a hue and cry, well over thirty convicts
downed tools and chased and caught the frightened
animal, tearing it to pieces in the act and eating it then
and there.

A couple of startled cranes flew overhead . . . and
still the warder chewed and spat.

The young white doctor at the native hospital,
charmingly kind but harassed with the heat and lack
of funds for medical necessities, seemed pleased to
speak to someone " almost straight from home."
He took my temperature. It was 100 degrees and
must have been so for some time.

" A touch of low fever, that's all. . . . I think I
will give you an injection," he said.

After a hurried consultation with his assistant, an
Indian native doctor, he apologised for the complete
absence of any kind of needle, except one which his
assistant had borrowed from the veterinary surgeon

43

three days ago. The hospital had run out of needles, and no fresh supply had yet arrived. The vet.'s needle was an outsize meant for cattle ; it looked out of all proportion to me ! After I had taken my quinine neat and discussed my ailments and he in his turn had talked of the hospital and the country as a whole, he leaned back in his cane chair, looked me up and down and said : " You know, I hate to say so, but I strongly suspect you're going to have a baby."

The words were said almost mockingly, and I took them in that spirit. But we both knew that for the time being, considering the circumstances, the truth was nothing less than a terrible blow. Presently the doctor took the calendar from the wall and after some hasty calculations said : " It will be just two months before Christmas. Now don't worry," he added, giving me a fatherly pat. " I'll come down to see you, if I have to ride on a donkey." (Alas, he never came, for when my time arrived he was already dead, having died suddenly of typhoid fever.) Almost adjoining the hospital was the smallest church I had ever seen. A perfect Gothic miniature built entirely of wood and straw. Being in the mood I went in, and sat down to gaze upon the painted altar, the golden crucifix and the hand-embroidered linen. I felt too tired to mind much about anything, even the baby. While I sat thus, partly dreaming and speculating that this little refuge was probably built through the proceeds of those boring church bazaars we used to hold (oh, so long ago) in Mannington, I heard someone calling from the sacristy. . . . Before me, a brightly painted Christ hung upon a cross with open arms. Two natives knelt there crossing themselves profusely, praying with intense fervour. What did they ask of God, I wondered, these favourite

44

children of His ? The coming of a child to them would hold no fear, physical or financial. Another native sat on the altar steps, his elbows on his knees, contemplating his toe-nails. Presently he took out a pen-knife and started to pare them. " Merengo," a voice called again from the sacristy, a white man's voice. The negro closed his pen-knife and rose. Slowly he turned, genuflected and went in the direction of the voice.

Just as I was leaving the church he returned and to my surprise asked me to follow him as the *Bwana*, his master, wanted to speak to me. I did not know his *Bwana*, but there in the gloom of the sacristy on a miserable stretcher-bed lay a man not unlike the wooden Christ on the Cross. Flushed and cadaverous, he stretched out an incredibly thin white arm to shake my hand.

" I'm Father O'Hara," he murmured.

His black eyes were bright with fever, but unlike those of the wooden image in the church, they twinkled merrily.

" Forgive me for calling you in," he almost whispered, " but I have been hoping for someone to come along all day. I'm a sick man as you see, and would very much like to dictate a letter—only a very short letter. . . . Would you," he smiled, " would you mind very much taking it down for me ? You see, the mail leaves to-night and Merengo cannot write. I tried to do it myself, but my hand's not very steady."

Merengo opened the door which led from the sacristy to the back of the church. Having disturbed a swarm of flies, he collapsed again in the shade of his hut to pare his toe-nails once more.

" There is some paper in that drawer, and a pen," said Father O'Hara. " There is also a manuscript," he added, with a twinkle.

The letter that he dictated was a short one, to his publishers in New York to whom he had sent some of his poems. The poetry, I noticed, was of a humorous kind.

" Sometimes," said the priest presently, " I get cheques for these things, which keep my mission above water. . . . This is the fourth mission I have started and put on its feet in twelve years. And never more than forty pounds in my pocket. . . ."

With a troupe of newly-converted natives, this Irish priest (the thirteenth son of a soldier) sets out literally into the blue and, choosing a likely spot where there is a river for preference, he and his flock begin to build some huts of straw. All that he needs are some tools, a few sacks of maize, medicine —quinine mostly—as well as a gun and some ammunition. Somehow, " with the grace of God," they managed to be fed, and lo ! in two or three years' time there stands a church, built of sunbaked bricks. " A labour of love, dear lady." So the mission is started, until eventually in full swing and entirely self-supporting, the church is left in charge of someone else and again the Irishman, after a short rest in the main mission—somewhere on the border of lake Victoria Nyanza—sets out to start another mission in a different part of the country ; teaching his men to build, to cobble, cook, read and write. Father O'Hara had come to Nymba to recuperate from the third attack of blackwater-fever, and his recovery, for the third time, was considered miraculous. He was still weak and his temperature was up, but he flatly refused to be sent home.

" There was so much to do," he sighed. " Only this morning two of my flock died of plague and I wasn't with them in their last hour." " No," he assured me, " I shall never go home again. There are thirteen iron crosses in the little cemetery behind that mission on the border of the lake, and I know mine will be the next. Besides, to tell you the honest truth, the more I see of white people, the more I like the black ones."

This charity, this labour of love and superhuman self-sacrifice! How much more it was needed to relieve the misery of the poor and unemployed—at home. I wanted to say so, but Father O'Hara was too ill. He now seemed too exhausted to speak. . . . I had not told him who I was or where I had come from, nor did he seem interested. After all, I was only white.

He thanked me with his eyes, and as I left the church he sent a native after me with a little gift. It was a copy of the *Imitation of Christ*, a much-used booklet, minus a cover. It was all that the Father had to give me, so the native said. I was very reluctant to take it and was about to return it, when the boy put his hands behind his back and said : " The master not needs books now, he knows it in his head, all of it, completely."

From the church door I had a view of almost the whole of Nymba. I could not see a single tree except those planted by the municipality leading from the hotel to the tiny court-house. It was, indeed, a barren plain ; there was in the air a homelessness which every sensitive White must have felt at times—especially if his outlook had been slightly jaundiced with malaria. I had the wind against me. The dust from the bazaar blew heavenwards, although it had rained in the night. Back at the hotel I found to my joy that the European mail had arrived. There was a gushing letter from a woman friend." Your letter," she wrote, " sounded like a fairy tale ! How I envy you. I imagine your lives are just one big adventure. I felt very lonely after you had gone ; some people, I

47

thought, have all the luck." It was extraordinary, I mused, how wrong people invariably were about the lives of others. . . .

Other White people were sitting on the hotel verandah, along with their letters and their thoughts ; poles apart from their environment and each other. The barefooted stewards closed the bar. The cane chairs creaked, two young ex-University men were talking of the everlasting topic of crops and rainfall. The pepper trees rustled softly ; the prison-clock struck ten. This clock was a primitive affair and a native sounded the hours by striking a hammer against a crowbar, which hung suspended from a beam. The fellow struck the quarters and then the hour, slightly varying the tone. (The actual time he took from the policeman's wrist watch !) Like Big Ben to the Londoner, the crowbar was Nymba's habitual companion. Only once, I was told, had the hours not been sounded for a day or two. This was when all the prisoners and the whole of the police force, excepting the white superintendent, had been down not with malaria but with measles. Measles being to them a comparatively new disease, introduced by Europeans, they " took it " very badly.

An elderly man in a wheel-chair, who had been wheeled out of the hotel-bar by the stewards, was now fast asleep. He whimpered plaintively like a child. A year ago he had lost both his legs through gangrene, but his people at home did not yet know. To-day he, too, had had some letters which brought the cool air of Scotland to his mind. He would never, he knew, go back there again. . . . He lay dreaming the uneasy dreams of a man who has faced worse things than death.

" Mac's got a nightmare," said a young man. " Wake him up."

48

" Why wake him ? " replied another. " It's a nightmare either way."

" He's drunk," said a third. " He's always drunk on mail-days. He goes and bullies the Goanese clerk till he hands him his mail long before office hours ; and then when he gets it, off he goes to get drunk."

" The best thing he can do," said the youngest of the party.

" He was a fine man, once," said the manager of Nymba's Grand Hotel.

In an isolated place like Nymba there is always the need for a little " romance " amongst the European population. It is often created by the mind to alleviate boredom. Sometimes, alas, it is mistaken for the real thing.

Nymba's one and only bachelor, one of the junior members of the White constabulary, had in turns been the darling of nearly every woman in the place. He was always " on " or " off " with some woman or another. I, too, had been singled out by him, for he sent me a bunch of violets after I had met him only once. They were outsize violets, grown in his garden, and were entirely deprived of scent by the tropical sun. Although only twenty-six, his hair was nearly white—the outcome, as he told me, of two years in the loneliest outpost on the Abyssinian border. For two years he had not seen a White man ; had at times been in danger of his life, gone short of food and been laid low with fever. He had lived a life so completely alone with his own soul that one might have thought it would have entirely changed his sense of values, his outlook on life, and given him enough philosophy to last him for a lifetime. But he returned to Nymba the same slightly effeminate snob that he had always been.

" Oh dear me no, I could never drink tea from an

earthenware pot," he remarked to me one afternoon. " I don't know how you can keep clean with that," he observed to me another time, pointing to a small canvas bath I had bought for myself. " Goodness me ! " he is said to have remarked to the wife of his superintendent as he caressed her, fingering a scrap of undervest which showed above her blouse, " it isn't silk."

# VIII

ON THE LAST NIGHT THAT I SPENT AT NYMBA, I
sat on the creaky bed in my barren room, sewing
baby clothes and trying to make up my mind whether
I should tell John of this coming child—or to wait a
little longer. He had so many other things to worry
him. I had just finally decided to wait till we were
properly settled on the farm, when there was a knock
at the door. A very pretty young woman, dressed
in white riding breeches, stood on the threshold,
introducing herself as Mrs. X.

" Lord, what a stink," she said as she collapsed on
the other bed, the only place there was to sit.

The " untouchable " had again drenched every
conceivable vessel with disinfectant. It hit you like
a wall at first ; it filled one's whole system, until one's
food, even one's cigarette seemed to taste of it—and
then gradually one grew accustomed to it.

" It's a wonder you don't get gassed," said my guest,
carefully lighting a cigarette. " By the way, I've
come to ask you to my party to-night, here at the
hotel. *Do* come—everybody will be here."

Mrs. X was reputed to be extremely unconventional and very wealthy. Her husband had several
thousand acres under cultivation, within a few miles
of Nymba. His place was fairly swarming with
tractors and the most up-to-date implements. Every
now and then, when there was a drought in South
America, he made a fair profit, so it was said,

51

unless of course there was a drought in Kenya as well.

" All right," I answered, " I'd love to come."

" Righto," she smiled, " let's be merry if we can. I haven't been drunk for months. The strain is beginning to tell."

Waited on by tall barefooted Goanese who were dressed in white, with red sashes, we were served with *hors d'œuvre*, soup, fish from the coast, mutton chops with mint sauce. We had cocktails, wine and brandy.

There was the Bank Manager with his anxious little wife ; one or two business men's wives ; several farmers' wives, all young with only two babies between them. Our hostess, who was now in high spirits, started the fun by throwing a chop at a steward's head. Her aim was good. He picked it up and carried it away with great dignity. He did not smile. She then threw another chop at Freddie, the darling of the ladies. Potatoes were next thrown, syphons were squirted and then, when meringues were served, the real battle began. Mindful of the only frock I possessed, I retreated like a coward and walked out into the road. Peeping through the blinds and believing themselves unobserved, several natives were watching the amazing battle which raged within. Opposite the hotel, still lit up, was the " Railway Club." It looked bare and was rarely frequented, reminding me of an isolation hospital. The permanent-way Inspector and another minor official were having a silent game of billiards. I don't know who was supposed to belong to this club, but I never saw a single woman there. They stayed at home, as did the wives of minor shopkeepers. . . .

Returning to the dining-room I found the battle over and my hostess in tears. Freddie, his white dinner-jacket soiled with gravy, was patting her on the back. The excitement had been too much for her ; or perhaps, after all, she had found it had not been so much fun as she had anticipated. . . . She was only a child, and she made me suddenly feel old.

Going into my Jeyes'-infected room, I found John there fast asleep. Leaning against the wobbly wash-hand stand was his bicycle on which he had ridden thirty miles. It was caked with mud and so were his shoes. At last, I sighed, our life together had begun and I was happy.

# IX

LEAVING NYMBA STATION, OUR COMIC LITTLE TRAIN, called Uganda Railway, chugged noisily uphill. We passed the native hospital, a compound of huts surrounding a bungalow, and then came to grass country and utter darkness. It was nearly midnight. The train on its daily run to the coast was taking us to Naituka where we had to attend a cattle-sale. Puffing along for several hours, we at length arrived at our destination between two and three in the morning. It was now moonlight, luckily, or else we should but with difficulty have found our way. A joy-riding rabble of natives shouted happily from the carriages in front ; whilst standing by the Indian station-master holding a kerosene lamp was a native dressed in a white shirt which hung outside his trousers. On his cap, embroidered in red lettering, was the name of the hotel. We decided to follow the boy. . . . Up we went over rocks and ant-hills, for apparently there was neither road nor footpath. Our porter had taken a short cut to save time. Luckily, however, the so-called hotel was not far away, and when it came into view we discovered that it was entirely built of wood and looked exactly like the cheaper kind of seaside bungalow. Stepping on to the latticed verandah which was faintly lit with a paraffin lamp suspended from the ceiling, I noticed several men lying on the floor apparently fast asleep. The same sight met our gaze in the dining-room and in the little lounge. Suspicious by experience, I thought that they were drunk ; but this time I was wrong. The place was simply overcrowded owing to the forthcoming sale.

It was indeed an eerie night : the air was strangely chilly in that altitude. The manager, looking pale, tired and terribly thin, showed us our room, which we had luckily booked by wire the day before. The room was almost similar to the one we had at Nymba, only it faced towards the back. In one of the huts at the back, the annex, I could see a White woman writing at a table, a candle illuminating her white face, which looked strangely spiritual like an Italian Madonna. The manageress, an Irishwoman, still doing her books at this unearthly hour. . . . At length John turned down the kerosene lamp which by now had attracted several different species of moths. In the quietness of the night I heard the breathing of the men outside the door. In the room to our right, separated from me by an inch-thick " wall," a man snored heavily and hit the partition at frequent intervals. Bang it went, and then the snoring ceased for a while, to be resumed a little later.

Shortly after dawn we were awakened with the usual cups of tea, a stimulant without which, it seemed, no one could possibly begin the day. Men were already queueing for their breakfasts, others stood on the verandah shaving, a few of them remained unshaved. The man who had slept on my right turned out to be a Jew, the only Jew at the sale, a friendly curly-headed young fellow, who sat at our table eating porridge.

" A good crowd," he said very cheerfully, rubbing his chubby hands.

" Yes," said John, eating his bacon and absorbed as usual with mental arithmetic.

55

"Would you," said the Jew, addressing me, "care to see my wool before the sale begins?"

His wool? "What wool?" I asked, feeling very ignorant.

"Sheep's, of course, madam," he smiled. Always willing to learn, I followed the man shortly after breakfast, leaving John to have a preliminary look at the cattle, of whch I suspected he was no judge. We walked down to the station, using the same short cut as the native had taken us the night before. By the goods shed stood half a dozen trucks filled to the roof with wool, which my companion had bought from the sheep-farmers of Naituka and distant surroundings. Proudly he slid the door open and proudly he showed me how tightly it was packed. There was something very childlike in the pride of this young Jew. He simply had to show his wool to someone, and possibly no one else would have been interested. He made annually, he told me, a good two thousand pounds clear profit. Every two years he went home and had a marvellous time in London.

"I wouldn't be a farmer for the world. Imagine me," he grinned, "pigging it in one of these God-forsaken places, worrying about the rainfall, chasing the sheep through the dip every day and sitting on a fence counting them afterwards."

Feeling rather depressed that this easy profit should go into this man's hands, a fellow who never even needed to grow up, a man who had to take no risks, I left him still fingering his wool. Making a *détour*, I passed a pretty cottage on the way. An old lady stood by the gate, hatless, white-haired and shrivelled. In a country where one so rarely sees old people, or even a choice of flowers, I felt curious about her. As I stopped by the fence to admire her well-kept little garden, she came up to me. By all appearances she was a rough diamond. Having seen me talking to the Jew, she thought that perhaps I needed a lecture.

" Young woman," she said, " mind these fellows. I've seen more white women go to the dogs in this country than I care to say."

" It's all right," I laughed, " I'm not going that way, There are other ways, though, it seems to me that one might go to the dogs in this country."

" Drink," she said laconically.

" No, not that."

" There ain't no other ways," she said with finality.

" Oh, yes, there are ! There is failure for one thing ; making no profits ; letting the other chap make the profits. . . ."

" Come, come, money ain't everything ! Let me show you some of my photographs. Come in, do."

Inside the humble little home I was shown the most interesting snapshots I have ever seen. They were even better than any of the films which had been shown during the last few years at home ; and what was more, they were genuine.

" You see," she went on, " I was practically the first White woman in East Africa. Forty-odd year ago I came here with my man. These wild animals, which you see in these photographs, used to be quite tame in those days. They weren't scared of people then. Just look at this leopard on the zebra's back—I took that at only twenty yards' distance. . . . These," she pointed to a box full of equally interesting, but very faded photographs, " used to be my most valued possessions, but now these foreigners come along with their paraphernalia and expensive cameras, and I'm afraid these pictures have lost their value to the likes of you. Times aren't what they were," she sighed, fingering her bits of cardboard. " Those were the days ! Time and again we could have made a fortune—time and again. We could have had the country for the asking, but we didn't. It don't matter now ; I'm old and I like it here."

There were many things I wanted to ask the old soul, but her mind seemed to have slipped into the past. I left her sitting with the yellowed snapshots in her lap, sunk in dreams of bygone days. . . . How she must have hated the intrusion of shipload after shipload of white people who have since robbed her of her own importance.

The galvanised-iron roofs of Naituka shone cheaply in the sun. Some wild pigeons gathered cooing on the hotel roof. There, under some trees in a rocky meadow, talking in groups stood several dozen white men and a handful of Somalis who had, together with their oxen and cows, trekked all the way from Abyssinia to sell their stock. They must have walked four hundred miles to try to obtain a better price for their cattle than they could have got at home. Time to them was of no importance. Here, as at Nymba, the white men were mostly of the public-school type. Two of them had brought their wives. Few of them, I reckon, had been born to farming. A young man stood talking to John :

" This place in the dry season is like a waste," he said.

It was, however, fairly green now, owing to recent rains, and the calm waters of the lake shone like a sheet of glass. A hippopotamus had chased the fellow who was talking to John that very morning. Having gone out in a boat, he just managed to out-distance the angry brute by a few seconds. Cambridge had won !

" This is a sheep country," said another young man to me.

58

He had, so he said gone to an agricultural college in the Midlands before coming out to Kenya. " I spent a small fortune bringing out a herd of pure-bred cattle with me from home, but they could not stand the climate. I was forever nursing them and now they arc all gone. East-coast fever mostly. . . . I ought to have known better," he added. " That's a half-bred over there," he said, pointing out a small cow which had just been led into the ring. " She was sold for three pounds. Now that one over there is three-quarter-bred," he said, when another beast came in. " They are pretty tough."

" Did you," I asked him, " find your education useful out here ? '

" Not much," he replied, " it's all so different. With the money I have spent and the work I have done, I would have done better at home. It's also the altitude up here that gets you. Ten thousand feet above the sea . . . on the equator it is no joke. Still," he smiled, " we manage. I'm thinking of going in for pigs because local consumption is going up steadily. It doesn't do, you know, to have all one's eggs in one basket."

The native cattle which the Somalis sold were very poor and the udders of the half-pint-a-day cows were practically non-existent. John bought a team of sixteen oxen and four native cows for our household milk supply. He also ordered some pigs to be delivered in a few weeks' time. The cows were barren, and the oxen badly trained—but this we only found out later ! Realising the many things that we did not know and should have to learn, I felt a little frightened. Forever trying to benefit by other peoples' experiences —especially by their mistakes—I realised how easy it was to lose one's money. Our capital, dwindling as it was, we simply dared not lose. It was our all.

59

The sale was nearly over and a couple of hundred weary oxen and cows, looking thin and underfed, were now being sorted out. An enormous flock of wild ducks had gathered on the water of the lake.

" It would be grand," said a young farmer to another, " to blaze at them ; why, you could get fifty of them with one shot."

He seemed to regret the lost opportunity, for his eyes wandered off to the lake during the whole of the sale. He was an eager young man, like most of them, about twenty years old. Occasionally there was some applause, if a particularly fine specimen of half-bred bull was brought into the ring, yet the young man's eyes invariably rested on the lake. He, I knew, found Kenya to be the paradise it was supposed to be.

When the bellowing and shouting of the market was over and many an old Ford, after some cranking, had driven off, the hotel filled once more. Everybody had another drink or two and then these men and few women went away, too, on horse-back, mule-back, ox-wagon, car or lofty gig. The one and only road which led through Naituka wound its way through the scattered little township, over the horizon into the distant blue. It went on for miles through lonely-looking country, where there was, from where I stood, no visible cultivation—nothing but barren hills, bare patches of rock and reddish earth. Back at the hotel waiting for the train to take us again to Nymba, from where we were setting out at last to our future home, John took out his pocket-book to reckon out our exact financial position. We now possessed—after buying the most vital necessities— exactly £500. " I had hoped," said John with his usual optimism, " to have more working capital, but this will have to do. After all, our living expenses will be almost *nil*."

I had not told him yet about the coming baby.

" Would you care to engage a Masai ' herd ' ? " asked the hotel manager after lunch. John having heard of the splendid qualities of the Masai, looked the native over as he stood on the doorstep, for he needed a ' herd ' almost at once. Someone had to mind the oxen, get them in the trucks to Nymba by the night train and lead the team out into the Simba valley. John was glad to get a Masai, for they were splendid cattle-men. He was a fine-looking negro, slim and upright, his plaited hair moist with oil and red with clay. His calm and dignity were as good as any White man's. His speech was " yes " and " no," nothing more.

" There aren't many Masais to be had," said the manager.

" All right," said John, and then to the negro, " Your work begins to-day." The Masai saluted and went off to sit by our oxen in the shade of a thorn bush. Usually the Masais stayed at home in their reserves and lived their own lazy lives as much as possible. Like the White man, they preferred being left alone and hated to be made to do things ; above all, they did not like work. Warlike by temperament, they felt suppressed. Having, like all natives, to pay a small tax, they either had to sell some cattle in order to pay or else to go out to work. Easier still it was to go out and raid the cattle, in order to pay, for they were not so easily found out. Occasionally the chief was made responsible for their misdeeds.

" Look here," says some young A.D.C. straight out from Oxford to some hairy chief. " We want some men to work for us."

" Indeed, sir," replies the chief, " you shall have some men when you need them ; but as you know, we don't hold with work. We hate it."

" Ah," says the A.D.C., " no work, no money."

" Money," says the chief, " we do not want it."

" But hang it all," retorts the young official, " everybody has to work. I have to work."

" Indeed you do, sir," answers the chief politely, and grins. There is something behind that grin which is infuriating. The A.D.C. controls his feelings ; there is no telling what he would like to do. The situation requires diplomacy. . . .

This particular Masai stayed with us for five years ; he was a faithful friend. Not being agriculturists, Masais live mainly on the flesh and blood of cattle. Their actual knowledge of cattle, however, is not so good as it is supposed to be. Our ' herd's ' diagnoses in the case of disease were often times slightly wild. If an ox was " blown " with colic and looked like dying, the Masai—accurately at times—made an incision with a knife. A nail would do just as well if a knife were not handy, and thus occasionally the beasts were relieved. Sometimes though, his aim was not so good . . . but the ox would have died anyway.

# X

H AVING RETURNED TO NYMBA THE NIGHT BEFORE, we were now ready to leave for our destination. Our wagon had been loaded high with our goods and chattels. For three solid hours John, the Masai, a *toto* (youth) and our houseboy belaboured the oxen till they were docile enough to be harnessed to the wagon. Weary and perspiring, John fetched me from the hotel yard. " Be quick," he said, " before they get entangled again." Waving good-bye to the manager, who refused to let us settle our account, we set off. His excuse was that he had not yet done the books ; and anyway, nobody paid until he sent in an account. It wasn't done. One's credit, I found, was always good ; nobody was supposed to be poor and everybody paid up—eventually.

So we rode out beneath the cloudless sky . . . to the most amazing solitude.

Up we went slowly, then down into the heat of the Simba valley. For the rest of the day I never saw another house, or a single stretch of cultivation. There wasn't even a tree. It seemed a magnificent landscape—from the distance ; but near at hand it was barren, utterly dry, soundless, almost hostile. Everything was bare : the table-top hills, the distant crater, the volcanic earth. Hopelessness personified. John and I, however (for such is youth), felt far from being depressed. Life was not so bad after all, I cogitated, as I sat on the covered wagon, comfortably

63

leaning back in our one and only arm-chair. It was not a real arm-chair ; it was made of canvas, an elaborate affair of red and blue stripes.

We seemed to be well on our way. The oxen pulled more evenly and thus we could enjoy comparative comfort. John was walking ; he liked walking. The Masai cracked his whip with great skill, and frequently he spat—another feat which he performed with equal perfection. The houseboy flourished a stick and the *toto*, too, who led the oxen by a rope in front, seemed happy. Later John unhitched his bicycle, which was attached in the rear, and rode for a change—clinging with one hand to the wagon. We had some rain in the afternoon which freshened things up—besides giving some hint of still better days to come. A distinctly promising influence, we felt, was in the air ; life was beginning to be exciting.

What tiny specks we must have looked in the eyes of the vultures which flew overhead in this vast vista of a barren plain ! John had his gun tucked away somewhere at the back of the wagon, in case he came across some antelope. The temperature was rising again ; the rain was over. My limbs were somewhat cramped, but I did not mind, for now our Great Adventure had begun. . . .

The *toto* was singing and his song in some strange way reminded me of the landscape. Utterly devoid of tune, it somehow resembled the chanting of the monks in Mannington's monastery. John looked absorbed and very happy astride his bicycle, puffing his pipe, and his blue eyes turned to the far north— our destination. The silence was almost uncanny. There was no bird-song, no sign of human habitation as far as the eye could see. We had now gone twelve miles—a good third of our journey—and it looked as though we would get through very comfortably.

Arriving at a stream, we decided to stop for the night ; to pitch our tent and throw some bushes together as a temporary enclosure for the oxen. The houseboy made a fire and was preparing to brew some tea. A cone-shaped hill on our left was a volcano, long extinct, which we decided to climb before it was dark. We wanted to look down from the peak into the abyss within, which we were told harboured every species of wild animal ; but all we saw was a wart-hog on the opposite side shyly peeping across the gulf. . . .

It is difficult to imagine a landscape so sombre and wild. Below we saw the curling flame of our camp-fire which was being nursed tenderly by the *toto*. Luminous creatures like will-o'-the-wisps hovered about, two to three feet above the ground. " Leopard's eyes," teased John, which I promptly believed. Then I asked the houseboy. Swahili is a limited language and he merely said " *dudah*," which means insect. Everything was a *dudah* from a mosquito to a cockroach. Fire-flies they must have been—yet even now I am not sure.

I awoke at 3 a.m. thoroughly chilled and bitten by mosquitoes. After a great deal of trouble I got the primus alight and made myself a cup of tea. Somewhere, far away, a hyena howled. I could not sleep again, and contented myself by listening to the oxen munching. The howling of the hyena came closer, then all was quiet again. The hours passed slowly until the dawn, which was to bring us to our much-dreamed-of home-to-be.

" Joan," said John as soon as he opened his eyes, " it will be grand next year to have the place all ship-shape, and a good crop of maize to tide us over every year till the coffee bears."

" Of course . . ." I agreed enthusiastically, thinking

how I was going to furnish the little place ; the pretty chintz curtains I was going to make ; the baby, the cot and the piano we might eventually buy.

" Even if I have to borrow money from the Bank," John went on, " it won't be much. I'll pay it back next year and then we'll buy a couple of mules and a buggy ; or perhaps a car if the road is fit for it."

The rising sun tipped the top of the crater. Our wagon was still in the shade below, sunk in a dreamy silence ; and then the sun shone brilliantly and the glory of the dawn disappeared into a uniform sameness of lightness and colouring.

It was not easy crossing a stream with a team of badly-trained oxen. I soon knew every swear-word in the Swahili language ! We had already wasted an hour and a half before the oxen were safely yoked to the chain. . . . The brakes seemed none too good. . . . We nearly crashed into the hindermost animals. Some chose to drink at this awkward moment, others got " unhinged." The water nearly reached the floor of the wagon, which was gradually sinking deeper into the river-bed. Just when the wagon had a list of 45 degrees the oxen stood still again. . . . I was feeling rather frightened as I gently slipped backwards on my chair. Then the front animals pulled once more ; the hindermost tugged backwards—a not very amusing tug o' war ! We coaxed in English ; we coaxed in Swahili. It was the first time that I had heard John swear ! Twice, one of the oxen lay down for half an hour. But he flatly refused to be coaxed, whilst as to having his tail twisted by an expert tail-twister (our Masai)— he was completely indifferent. The other oxen, thinking their task done, began to graze. They slipped out of their gear and wandered off in search of food and freedom. . . .

Suddenly the Masai asked for matches. Still being

very " English," John watched the fellow's preparations with some anxiety. The Masai collected firewood, a twig here and a twig there, and built it up beneath the beast. He then applied a lighted match. . . . Soon the fire burned merrily, yet the oxen refused to budge. There was an unpleasant smell of burning hair, of singeing flesh, and it looked as though the beast was content to let us roast it alive. Munching contentedly, the other oxen stood watching placidly, and John was just about to fetch a bucket of water to extinguish the fire when slowly and with amazing dignity the animal rose to its sturdy legs. . . . On we went again ; down, down, down, followed by four care-free cows. . . . The iron bedsteads rattled and banged ; the cooking-range looked silly, towering above me at the back of the wagon.

Gradually the scenery changed. The landscape grew more fertile and every hour or so we saw a house dotted here and there in the distance. Several maize and coffee plantations bordered on to the hole-ridden road. But we dared not stop, for fear of having further trouble with the oxen. Once, however, the hindmost beast did lie down, but John hit upon a novel idea this time. He covered the animal's nose and mouth with both his hands and in its struggle for breath, it rose to its feet again—and so the procession went on. Once we disturbed a snake which lay sunning itself in the middle of the road ; once, too, we met a solitary White man riding on a white mule, which promptly took fright as it approached our team. The mule fell into a hole and gently threw its rider. But the fellow didn't seem to mind.

" I have witnessed a land rush, a sisal rush, a coffee rush, a tea rush and a gold rush," he informed us, " but so far it was the land rush which had been the most profitable. Yet, surprisingly enough," he added, trying to sooth his fractious mule, " many of us did not profit by that, either. As a matter of fact, few of us had the foresight. . . . Ah, well," he said, remounting, " good luck to you ! "

The farms we passed were few and far between ; some were desolate-looking, others gave the impression of flourishing. Still we went down, the road gradually ceasing altogether to become a mere footpath. We crossed two more streams and, leaving plantations far behind us, we approached the lower Simba valley. Vultures swooped down from enormous heights. . . . Slowly we drove through a quivering heat which seemed almost alive, and after four more hours of difficult going we arrived by a shallow lake—a swamp, as it was called by most people.

" This," said John with a certain pride, " is our farm."

A flock of white pelicans withdrew momentarily from the water, to settle down once more in search of food. Flies buzzed and even stung. Some cranes flying overhead raised their raucous voices as if objecting to this new intrusion into their own province. They screamed persistently like cats in spring. Just in front of us, up an incline, with a stretch of forest at the back, stood a dark brown mud house with a corrugated-iron roof—a poor sort of place, resembling a neglected barn. I jumped off the wagon and gave a great sigh of relief. It was nice to be at home somewhere, anywhere, at last. The oxen, too, seemed to feel relieved as we removed their gear. We were met by some natives who had come to look for work, and were awaiting our arrival. Some had their wives with them ; calm-eyed women, pregnant every one, except the very old and very young. Even a cook was at hand, a perfectly murderous-looking fellow with but one tooth to light up his pockmarked face. Like an ape's, his enormous hands reached well below his knees. But he proved to be a godsend, a very good friend, indeed, in years to come.

"*Memsahib,*" he said before I had gone into the house, "I am a good cook. I will also make *memsahib* a cup of tea this instant. There is a good fire going at the back of the house." He then handed me a letter wherein was written : "Odero has worked for me for six months. He is a splendid cook, but he has become too big for his boots."

"Letter not much good perhaps?" Odero asked, "but I am a good cook. I will show you, please." Knock-kneed and ugly though he was, the fellow obviously had a heart of gold. Knowing full well that no White woman could possibly do her own cooking in the tropics, I engaged him.

Cracked though the walls of the three-roomed house were, they were a good eighteen inches thick. To me, it seemed a desolate sort of outpost, yet better than nothing. The incredibly coarse grass which grew right up to the doorstep almost rattled in the breeze. The place was littered with tin cans and other empties which had obviously been got rid of by just being thrown out of the door ! Nearly all the window panes were broken ; some of the gaps were filled with pieces of American cloth. There was no floor, no ceiling. The rafters above were festooned with cobwebs, and at my approach an enormous hairy spider fled into the darkness. . . . Hornets flew in and out ; some rotting animal-skins in the bedroom were alive with a strange species of brown, hairy maggots which crawled everywhere. A giant lizard fled up the wall, balancing on the rafters, to meet its mate aloft. The house seemed to be a perfect paradise for a naturalist, an ideal opportunity in fact, to study in one's home. In the large centre room—the sitting-room to be—was an old green plush arm-chair and an equally old gramophone with a few records on a bamboo table. . . .

John was already unloading the furniture. First came the table and then the chairs ; and then we indulged in a cup of tea and a slice of home-made bread which the cook had made in a petrol tin placed over an open fire. We both felt much more cheerful after this " meal." A pretty little stream sang by the house, friendly and comforting. The iron-roof of the house retained the burning heat of the day and it was much cooler to be outside than in. Soon the sun set like a dying flame—suddenly, without lingering.

Night fell, and soon the air was seething with hidden life. Mosquitoes rose from the swamp below ; moths fluttered wildly, as well as bats and other nameless things. The cries of strange animals came to my ears. . . . The oxen, which were driven into an enclosure of thorn-bushes, appeared restless and stamped their feet. They were due to go back to Nymba to-morrow in order to fetch the plough and the other implements we had left behind. The house-boy and the cook brought a bath of hot water to my room and placed it by the bed. It was a small affair and that part of me which was not under water was being unmercifully stung by mosquitoes. Joining John in the dining-room, where he had just killed a snake, I wound up the gramophone. The records were a good fifteen years old and of a sentimental kind. " The Tales of Hoffman," " Two Eyes of Grey," and " Somewhere a Voice is Calling." Deciding that none of them would suit the occasion and that the morning would bring forth fresh interests, we went to bed. It was only eight o'clock, but we were very tired.

Several times during the night I awoke with a start. Hyenas cried within a few yards of the house ; jackals raised their voices and still mosquitoes stung. . . . Somewhere in the world without, wild life was being lived beneath the stars ; a weird kind of life, the thought of which made me grateful when day broke. John was up at dawn, eager to start his work. What he was first going to do I did not know, inspanning the oxen I expected.

There were maggots crawling between my sheets, my face was swollen with mosquito-bites and a toad had hidden in my slipper. But to compensate for these horrors, the cook was as good as his word and his porridge and his poached eggs, his toast and his potato crisps, were fit for a queen. Proudly he served the food himself, waiting to be praised. The house-boy, having watched the hotel stewards during our stay at Nymba, had folded the table-napkins most artistically—but he also left his finger prints behind ! John rang the farm-bell at 7 a.m. and the men trooped happily to work, shouting and singing. There were sixty of them, many more than we could afford, but we needed them. . . .

It was now April nearly gone and coffee should have been planted some time ago. Bushes were cleared, coffee-beds made by hand, beans planted— but we were just too late. By the time the coffee-beans had started to sprout, the dry season had already set in (prematurely we were told), and any amount of irrigation could not counteract the scorching sun, which caked the surface of the soil. Unable to lift their heads, the necks of the beans were scorched and withered. John and the boys scratched the ground like hens, trying to save the saplings, but few survived.

First and foremost, however, we planted maize—

almost in the rear of the plough, as it was now nearly too late. We were obliged to feed the natives and so far had to buy their food. This had to be fetched, which meant taking oxen from the plough at frequent intervals. The short rains, which were said to follow the long ones, did not set in at all. Our first little crop of maize was but a dwarfed affair, but by discharging half the men, we just managed to keep the rest in food.

Opening the ground was slow work as there was an amazing number of bushes to be cleared as well as thorn-trees to be felled, before we could hitch the oxen to the plough. The labourers on our farm were mostly from the Kikuyu country, all of them wearing their native attire which consisted of a once-red cotton-blanket fastened to the left shoulder and sandals made of zebra hide.

The natives' huts, which were built of straw, were also shared by all their possessions—goats and hens and even calves. Yes, it was but yesterday that these people were fierce and warlike, and now they let themselves be driven. They were a cheerful lot as a whole and far less to be pitied than the White man. The house was being whitewashed inside and out by the houseboy, the cook having discovered a patch of lime somewhere. We made a " ceiling " in the sitting-room by stretching yards of American cloth from wall to wall, hoping thus to stop those sickening thuds caused by insects and small animals falling from the rafters which we heard in the dead of the night.

John now knew of the coming baby. He was glad, he said. " Next year we shall be able to buy all we need for you and the kid."

My sitting-room looked very pleasing. The home-made sideboard filled my heart with pride, but the difficulty was how to stop it from wobbling. . . .

There was my silver teapot, the pride of the house-boy, hobnobbing with a bottle of whisky—a luxurious bottle of whisky which we bought in case of snake-bite or any other emergency. We cleared the grass outside the house and added a verandah, an extra foot of mud which I covered with coconut matting. John planted a row of eucalyptus trees all round the house, the pungent smell of which was supposed to keep mosquitoes away. We had no vegetables as yet, but the cook found a place where some wild spinach grew and spinach we ate every day for several months until our own stuff matured.

John ploughed for hours and felled trees single-handed. He was building an enormous store with a thatched roof which was to house his future crops of maize. I hoped that some day he might grow enough to fill it. Up till then we had still to buy some from an old Scotch woman who lived by her-self several miles away. Her maize was old and full of weevils, but the natives did not seem to notice them. Several times the carrier brought some cheese from the same woman—sour milk, gone rancid, pressed through a strip of muslin. Thinking it was a present, I was shocked to get an account on the first of the month for two shillings per cheese.

"Two shillings!" I exclaimed to John. "Why, it was so bad that we couldn't even eat it!"

Next time the carrier brought a cheese I politely returned it. I never knew whether it was the returned cheese, but the Scotch woman hated me at sight! She was old, I was young. She seemed to have no heart for youth, but she had a passion for her dogs. Her yellow, wrinkled face, hard and cold, was like a man's. She dressed like a man ; rode, hunted and swore like a man. She was a marvellous shot, so we were told, and had killed lions single-handed. I had seen her

73

pluck ticks from the flee-ridden coats of her pack of dogs, and wipe their eyes with her handkerchief. . . .

One day she was telling John about her bitch which was on heat again, and of her quarter-bred bull which might be loaned at so-and-so much per cow. . . . Her manager, a young man about twenty-six, red-cheeked and round-eyed, seemed effeminate by comparison, and as she mounted her mule and cantered away, I heard her shout to her manager who rode behind, " Lord help me, that b—— fool actually blushed ! " This was the last time that I saw her. She never called again, nor did we buy another cheese or any further maize from her.

Another farm to the east of us, some four miles away, was managed by a bachelor of sixty. He had an enormous herd of cattle and several acres under maize. He was said to be a recluse. Having lived in dire solitude for many years, his instinct was to hide at the approach of any other White man. So socially our valley was, indeed, a washout. The man was kind though and sold us all the maize we needed, and loaned us his bull for half the price the Scotch woman had asked. Alas, he did not live long after our arrival. The natives found him shot dead on New Year's Eve. His predecessor, we were told, had also taken his life in the same way two years ago. . . .

# XI

I WAS LYING ON MY BED WITH MY EYES CLOSED, listening to the crack of the driver's whip, the gurgling stream and the metallic screech of the plough. The clanking of the plough-chains brought John to my mind—toiling out there for Heaven knew what. The sun had cracked the earth and I could see whirls of dust blowing sky-high. The houseboy came running in to say that someone was coming up the path on a mule ! The nurse had arrived, a white nurse whom I had managed to secure after a great deal of correspondence. She was Australian and fairly used to the bush. She had spent seventy-two hours on the road, sleeping at nights in the tiny tent which was fastened behind her on the mule. Her servant, carrying her suitcase on his woolly head, followed her.

She sighed as she dismounted the somewhat under-sized mule, and stroked its head. Plump and middle-aged though she was, nothing it seemed unduly frightened her except inactivity. For a whole fortnight, having come too soon, she groused at the primitiveness of the place—the lack of this, the lack of that ; the heat, the insects and the sand-fleas which were all too plentiful.

" No ceiling," she cried in horror, " why, you'll get sunstroke indoors ! " " Good lord, haven't you any mosquito nets ? " or " You'll have to have a wooden floor now baby is coming."

" Is this supposed to be a cot ? " she asked, viewing

a home-made structure which looked none too steady on its legs. She had never been to a place quite like this before, her previous patients having been far more well-to-do. I felt sorry for her.

She should have been sorry for me, but that never occurred to me at the time. I felt guilty and apologetic. "Let's see the baby's clothes," she ordered. After tea, feeling guiltier than ever, I produced some garments I had made during the last few months. "Are these," she demanded, pointing to the modest little collection of clothes, "meant for a baby or a doll?"

Looking the little clothes over myself once again, I too felt as though they had somewhat shrunk, they certainly seemed too small. . . .

Nothing, I realised, would cheer the nurse except the arrival of the baby. One morning at the break of dawn she sent the houseboy off to Nymba to fetch the doctor, who had promised to come some time ago. The houseboy was the only negro who could be trusted to ride John's bicycle. Sending John out on his twice-weekly pursuit of food, in order to get him away, we waited for the doctor's arrival, hoping that with luck he might arrive by tea-time. His Ford, we reckoned, would easily manage the trip now that the rivers were low and the paths were dry.

He never came, but the natives from neighbouring farms, as well as our own, flocked together in the hut of the cook which stood some fifteen yards from the house. How they knew of this coming event was impossible to tell, but they oftentimes appeared to *sense* such things. . . . For hours after sunset they sat in the dark, twanging their guitars. *Twang*, *twang*, and the refrain ; the same eternal tune until midnight, when my daughter Marie was born.

I heard a Kikuyu shriek the news into the night as though he wanted to tell the stars. It was midnight, according to the nurse's wrist-watch. Hers was the only timepiece in the house. On the whole we did not need a clock, finding it easy to read the hour by the sun ; time in any case was almost of no importance in this far-away existence.

The baby did not seem to want to live at first. The nurse, old-maidish though she was, seemed to be amazingly resourceful. Taking the infant by her wee legs, she started to swing her about until the nurse's face shone with perspiration. There was, of course, little enough room to swing a child. I closed my eyes . . . and too tired to mind anything very much, I fell asleep. The last sound I heard before losing consciousness was the feeble wailing of my baby. . . .

John, who had wandered up and down the verandah half through the night, crazed with anxiety, came to greet me in the morning. He looked as if he had for the first time in his life come across some real hardship. The houseboy returned at dawn with a letter from Nymba's new doctor. " Sorry," it ran, " but I'm quite unable to come. In any case, I should probably arrive too late. I am told, too, that your road is quite impassable by car. . . ."

Little Marie was a good baby ; easy to rear. Her arrival created great excitement amongst the workers, who had never seen a white baby before. How curious they were, how they peered in at the window in the hope of getting a glimpse of something that was to them so very ordinary and yet so very different—a baby of a different colour ! They brought gifts of bananas, of charms and gourds of wild-honey. The entire population of the near-lying forests and the other white men's farms clustered round our house to see this white " piccannini."

77

The nurse held the baby high above her head for them all to see. Some Vaderobos spat, a sign of veneration ; the others just looked at the struggling mite without a word. A Vaderobo chief came forward with an incredibly verminous cheetah-skin as a gift. Having presented themselves to us and duly admired the baby, something had to be done in return. They all seemed hungry. Our store of maize was running low, and not having grown sufficient even to feed our own people we could not afford to be very generous. The Vaderobos also asked for matches, for to them matches were the only desirable thing that the White man's civilisation had so far produced. . . .

The baby was barely ten days old when the nurse left in order to fulfil another pressing call. She did not like leaving me as my temperature was still up to 100 degrees and I was barely able to stand. Sitting comfortably in the wagon which was to take her back to Nymba, her head bumped against a swarm of wild bees as the wagon was passing beneath a tree. Screaming wildly she jumped off the cart and ran back into my room, where I still lay on my bed. Bees swarmed furiously about her, bees settled in her hair ; bees, indeed, buzzed angrily everywhere, and she was being badly stung. Luckily she wore a wig, which she tore from her head and dropped into a jug of water, and it was a poor wet wisp that she eventually withdrew from the jug to dry in the sun before she again prepared to depart. This tragi-comic episode had given her a nasty shock and she was slightly annoyed with me—for after all, the discomforts she had endured were caused through me. Off she went once more, her mule following behind the wagon —and I was left alone. Not really alone, of course, for there was the child which required my every attention. Slowly I got dressed; clinging dizzily to the bedstead. . . .

Trying to rear a child with cows' milk is not always easy. The greatest trouble I experienced after the nurse had left was the feeding problem, as I had no feeding bottle and no teat. One of our cows had calved, but the other three we had found were useless, in spite of the loan of our neighbour's bull. Feeding the baby with a spoon, sterilizing the milk, boiling and filtering the water, as well as washing her clothes, was all that I was able to manage. I now weighed only 7 stone as compared with 9 stone when I had left home, whilst I had a temperature every night for six months after the baby was born. Luckily the child thrived; but we were obliged to buy another cow, with a calf this time.

No sooner had the nurse departed, however, than the houseboy wanted to leave. The cook, too, wanted two months' leave in order to go back to his native reserve to buy a wife, for he had now saved up enough to buy a couple of cows or so, with which to make the purchase. In common with all men, and in spite of having but one tooth in his head and no physical attractions whatsoever, he insisted that his wife should be young, strong and good-looking! During his absence, an ordinary ploughboy was put to do the cooking. He had picked up the art in his spare time, when sitting in the kitchen with his friend the cook. He made a surprisingly good job of it.

Feeling desperately weak and almost unable to drag myself from bed to chair, I felt very grateful when a new houseboy arrived—a Christian like the cook, but not a Roman Catholic. I believe he wanted to convert me.

"Do you believe in God!" he asked me rather

79

accusingly one morning as he brought me some boiling water.

" Of course, Kamau," I said, " don't you ? "

" Is it true," he said, " that God is a *Mesungu* (a White man) ? "

Now this was a very difficult question to answer in Swahili, but I tried to make it clear that God was neither white nor black, but a spirit, a kind of " magic " in his language.

" Perhaps," he replied doubtfully, " but I think he likes the White man best."

Completely ignorant of the White man's burden, as all black men are, I told him that in reality the white man was no better off, in many instances not as well off as the negro.

" So we are brothers, white man and black man, just as the Missionary said ? "

" Of course we are ! " I assured him somewhat airily, for it is a delicate matter to discuss religion with a native—especially when one's own theology is a bit weak !

" Would you," he asked one evening, coming on to the verandah with an indescribably filthy garment in his hands, " mend my trousers, like you do the master's ? "

I had now become his sister, and the relationship was getting closer than I had intended. I compromised. " Take this needle and cotton," I coaxed, " and just try and do it yourself."

I was getting a little stronger when a native policeman arrived from Nymba headquarters with a letter telling us of a suspected invasion, a raid on White people by the Kamasias. This was a tribe which had settled not far from us ; indeed, I believe that we lived nearer their reserve than any other Europeans. Having been duly warned, John nevertheless went about as usual, while I accused him of lacking imagination. I frequently walked up to the hill-top where, lying down behind a hillock, I took out my field-glasses and viewed the horizon to the east—the danger quarter. Completely uninhabited as the district was, I missed nothing which suggested a sign of man ; not the slightest curl of smoke escaped me.

There were many other things I saw, too. Ostriches with bedraggled feathers parading stiffly by the lake ; zebras herding in the distance. John laughed at me when I suggested arrangements for a possible barricade and made sure that the guns were loaded. As time went on fear grew less, although the thought of a few hundred bloodthirsty savages, armed with spears and poisoned-arrows, weighed down my courage. How the Nymba police-department got hold of the rumour I do not know. Native gossip, perhaps. The Kamasias were not particularly trusted and, like the Masai, they did not work. It was the cattle they wanted which they stole whenever the opportunity presented itself. Cut-throats that they were by reputation, and probably by instinct, they despised the workers, the agriculturists.

Trouble was in store for us, however, when Odero the cook returned. He and his temporary successor had a terrible fight over some professional disagreement. Suddenly I heard a scuffle of feet and then a shout for help from Odero's young wife. John was away, and I ran to the back of the house to see a deadly-serious exhibition of all-in wrestling. It looked dangerous, especially as each man carried a knife. When I arrived I learned that cook No. 1 had bitten cook No. 2 in the face and blood was flowing down the victim's clothes. Snarling like furious dogs, they took no notice of me, in spite of my whip. I ordered the bride to fetch a bucket of water, which I told her to throw over the two men. Rather hesitantly she let fly and the lot of it struck her spouse, who promptly stopped the fight, turned and " biffed " his wife over the head. Crying loudly, the girl crept into their hut, while her husband came to me to have his lip stitched up. Cook No. 2 later presented himself to me to claim his wages and beg a letter of recommendation.

Odero's marriage was not the happy, placid affair of the average negro's married existence. He did not trust his wife ; he was forever spying on her, following her, accusing her, trying to catch her with another fellow. He was paying the penalty of having married a girl just half his age. She did not even bear him any children—another cause for complaint. The blame, of course, was also put on the hapless girl.

## XII

THERE WAS AN APPALLING SAMENESS ABOUT THE days and months. . . . John sat on the swaying plough in the fierce afternoon sun, urging the tired oxen on. The furrows grew uneven, the swaying team zigzagged drunkenly. To me, our life seemed a kind of penal servitude for some vague offence ; the sins of our fathers, perhaps. In such a frame of mind we spent our Christmas.

On Christmas Eve, almost the hottest day of the year, John had gone out to try to secure some meat or a few wild guinea-fowl for our dinner. The sun set and darkness folded the prairie in a kind of peace ; a bat circled wildly over my head as I sat on the verandah fretting over John's lengthy absence. At last he arrived with a single duck—the only thing he managed to bag. Our Christmas mail from home did not arrive until January. So laboriously we slipped from the old year into the new ; John toiling, I waiting. . . . At times it seemed to me a precarious kind of existence, yet the coming year was bright again with new hope and promise. Such is youth !

What made life seem less worthwhile was that we were not stripping the land of rocks and bushes ; were not, in fact, preparing the future for our children, as one might do at home. Tilling the land for a family to come would have certainly made our existence more worthwhile, but we did not want our children to remain here. In common with most settlers, we dreamed of ultimate success and then " home " before we were too old. It was in the evenings that we discussed again the things to come, yet lurking at the back of our minds was the horror of our dwindling capital. Having now reduced our staff to twenty men our progress was slow, whilst we had exactly £250 left to carry on for another six months or so, when the next crop of maize should be ready. We had now nearly ten acres ready, but progress was tardy with but one team of oxen and only a single plough. Three oxen died of East-coast fever ; luckily the rest of the herd proved immune.

# XIII

Magnificent the day would have been called in England, with brilliant sun and deep blue sky, when I took the baby for her first outing. Marie was now three months old and I carried her across my hip as I possessed no pram. (Not that a perambulator would have been much use on the farm.) Following a buffalo-track through the wood, I eventually arrived on the escarpment which I had so often seen from the distance. Sitting on a rock where I had a good view of the Simba valley below, the lake and John's team at work, I saw a lioness in front of me—not more than fifty yards away. With her were her cubs, three of them. She saw me too ; indeed, she had probably seen me for some time. Across a gulf of tall brown grass we stared at each other, she with her babies and I with mine. I don't know how long we regarded each other thus, but to me it seemed an eternity. I dared not move. Convinced, probably, that I was harmless, the beast then turned and slowly moved away. Whither she went I do not know, but I hastily left in the opposite direction to where I saw her last.

Discovering another track, I followed this for ten minutes or so when I came across the body of a Kikuyu woman lying face downwards across the path with an empty water-gourd on the ground beside her. At first I thought she was asleep. A thick cloud of flies rose from the spot as I approached whilst a couple of vultures circled high above. . . . Hastily retreating from the place, I arrived at the source of our stream and following it I soon arrived back on the farm.

Hastening to where John stood oiling the plough in the calm of the quivering heat, I told him about the lion and the corpse. He told the ploughboy, who told it to the ' herd,' who shouted it to the *shamba* boys. Making their voices carry like Alpine yodellers, they shouted the news to the houseboy—and within three minutes everybody knew. Koro, one of our *shamba* boys, asked to be taken to see the dead woman as he had an idea that she might be his mother. He had been expecting her to come to him from the Kikuyu reserve for some time. So up we went along by the gurgling stream, one behind the other, pock-marked Koro in the rear, none of us speaking till we reached the corpse. Koro would not go near ; he stood in the distance peering over my shoulder. But presently he said " Yes, this is my mother's gourd."

His grief was neither silent nor profound. Down Koro fled to the fields, shouting the news in all directions. Picking up his hoe where he had dropped it, the boy started to dig again while he sang a ditty about his mother, which he had made up on the spur of the moment. Indeed, why not ? I asked myself; for now—according to Koro—his mother was walking in the fields of heaven, surrounded by herds of cows and sheep, and shambas of ripening corn.

After sunset, the natives twanged their guitars. . . . Death was just an incident. I alone felt depressed— about the old woman facing it alone.

## XIV

J OHN HAD BEEN FELLING TREES TO BUILD A PIGSTY, driving the posts deep into the earth and joining them with branches, barbed-wire and surrounding the lot with a wall of thorn bushes. Then fourteen black piglets arrived together with an enormous boar—sent to us by a dealer from Naituka. Every blessed night, especially when the moon was high, those pigs worried their way out of their enclosure and went for walks. Into the maize-store, on to our verandah, even into the kitchen and the cook's hut they went grunting happily, munching the cook's failures which he had hidden in a box under the kitchen table.

In the middle of the night John drove them back to the enclosure. More bushes were added and further posts were driven in, until eventually their *boma* was completely "hog-tight." It was so solid a structure that we almost regretted it, for the very first night that the animals' wanderlust had been frustrated, a leopard jumped into the enclosure and ate the most promising young sow. Our 'herd' knew another 'herd' whose boss who lived ten miles away owned a lion-trap. John promptly asked if he might borrow it but the owner, a South African, insisted on presenting it to us. He had, so he said, more traps than he knew what to do with. In fact, they fairly littered up the place. John carefully set the contraption before he went to bed. The leopard duly returned, as leopards and lions always do, and was just going to help himself to another sow when he got caught by the leg above the knee-joint. The beast, almost too lovely to destroy, tried desperately to escape by biting through his own leg. Had John not finished him off at daybreak, he might well have escaped, minus a leg.

Our pigs, contented though they were, did not seem to fatten ; indeed, they were the leanest pigs I had ever come across. Their diet, which consisted principally of grass, was probably to blame. They were far too lively for pigs, I thought, calling to mind the enormous mounds of flesh which used to loll placidly at agricultural shows at home. Ours never lolled. They seemed amazingly prolific, though, and John was forever being called out to attend the birth of piglets, which if not protected were frequently eaten by their mother.

On one of those unbearably hot days, I came upon him squatting in the pigsty, engrossed in some mysterious surgical operation upon the youngest pigs. A great deal of shrieking was going on ; a fierce yell or two and then sudden silence.

" Whatever are you doing there ? " I shouted above the din.

Looking very hot and bothered, John wiped his blood-stained knife on his handkerchief, and then in a voice which sounded as though he had done nothing else all his life : " I'm only gelding the superfluous males."

" Good heavens," I cried, " who told you to do that ? "

" Oh, I've read it up somewhere, of course ; besides it's only commonsense."

Acting as assistant, the Masai was greatly impressed by John's surgical skill. I expected them all to die of blood poisoning, but their recovery was as perfect as it was rapid. After this, John's reputation as a surgeon spread. The natives suddenly wanted their teeth drawn. Almost all had bad teeth, as they were in the habit of filing them, which ruined the enamel. Trying to do extractions with pliers, John was not always successful. . . .

Never had I seen such teeth, for sheer length, as those of the average African. The operation was conducted by the negro lying flat upon his back and John kneeling on the fellow's chest. With another chap holding down the victim's head the struggle began. But sometimes the job had to be abandoned as hopeless. Later, however, when John had received a couple of pairs of forceps from his dentist at home he felt obliged to make a small charge per tooth drawn, for his fame as dental-surgeon spread beyond the valley and the steadily-increasing number of patients who turned up on Sunday afternoons seemed to warrant some sort of remuneration.

## XV

THE RAINS WERE LONG OVERDUE. ONE DAY, however, at the beginning of March they burst upon us—out of the blue. There was a dull dead calm, the wind had dropped and a patch of white cloud in the blue sky seemed stationary behind Laikipia. Gradually it grew larger. Suddenly, at midday, an enormous peal of thunder crashed over the valley whilst a blinding flash seemed to rend the heavens. . . . How profound the silence was again a moment after! The sky grew slowly dark, almost black; a wave of hot air moved over the earth and then enormous drops of rain fell heavily upon the iron roof of our house. Another flash of lightning and another peal of thunder, and then the tropical downpour began.

The water ran over the parched ground in rivulets. It beat against the house and slowly trickled on to the floor of our dining-room, forming a pool two inches deep. John came running in with his spade and hastily dug a trench behind the back door, so as to lead the water off. He was happy now ; the time for sowing had arrived. All things came to life again— both good and bad. Mosquitoes spread like wild-fire, toadstools grew inside the walls of our house and then I was taken ill with sciatica. Lying on my bed with the sheet pulled over my head, to protect myself from " things " falling from the rafters, I was in agony for two or three weeks.

The first green shoots of maize began to appear above the ground almost before I was up again. John had rushed off to Nymba to buy coffee seedlings. He wanted to plant at least five acres with coffee this season. It was not much, but as much as he could do ; and he seemed content. Unused to the fresh green grass, three oxen died of colic. This now left us only ten. . . .

The rain suddenly and unaccountably ceased. Frequently the clouds gathered behind the escarpment, only to disappear into the blue. " It's bound to come," John would say hopefully, looking up to the skies ; but again the clouds drifted away to the south. It was as if they were held back by an invisible hand, on the very brow of the hill. The seedlings wilted and then after a month of drought they died. The wilderness seemed untamable at times like these ; there was simply no response. . . . John patiently ploughed the field again, and then again it rained. Again we sowed, but having lost two months or more, our crop was not comparable with what it might have been. It would not carry us over for another year.

" Ah, well," said John, " it can't be helped. Next year, Joan, we will be all right."

Not once did his spirit, his courage or his hope flag within him. Forever he worked and planned anew.

" Next year," he remarked hopefully, " I shall have even more acres under cultivation ; at least double of what we have now. And then our profits will be really good. . . ." " Cheer up ! " he said on the day of our first anniversary on the farm, " we will show them yet ! " We had grown very economical, having as yet bought no clothes, no tinned foods and no alcoholic drinks. We still had only two gramophone records, and we still had no wooden floors.

The months ahead of us had few features really worthy of note. It was a period of waiting. The strain of the heat was unceasing, yet each day brought us nearer our goal.

It was during our second dry season that a native whose hut was only fifty yards from our house was taken very ill, but his friends did not tell me until he showed distinct signs of smallpox. He lay on a blanket outside his hut where his wives had carried him, every inch of his body covered with the most deadly spots. As he had been visited by all his friends and had shared the hut with his family, I expected the most appalling epidemic. None of us had ever been vaccinated, so once again the house-boy went to Nymba to fetch the doctor, but once again he returned without him. From inside his shirt he pulled out a small parcel with a note.

" I am sending you the vaccine. Please vaccinate everybody on the farm," the doctor wrote, "—men, women and children. It is quite simple : take a clean pocket-knife and with the back of the blade make three to four scratches on the person's arm, paint over with the vaccine, tie some muslin round, and then in a few days' time I will try to come down and see if it has worked."

Hateful though it was, it had to be done. It was at lunch-time when the natives had all lined up to be doctored, standing in a row, looking serious and ill at ease. I explained to them that this mysterious medicine in the tiny bottle was going to protect them from smallpox, but our patients looked completely indifferent. What did they care, they were superbly unafraid of death. Death is no tragedy to them ; it is not as though with a man's death someone lost their breadwinner. Still, they did as they were told without a question, but it was not till John promised them a holiday in three days' time that they looked more cheerful. I was feeling rather sorry for them. John washed their arms with disinfectant, made the scratches while I applied the vaccine and the bandages. There were seventy-five of them, including women and children. The little *totos* who looked up at me with trusting eyes, never even flinched. Proudly displaying the white strips of linen, practically the only thing they wore, they went back to their huts to roll in the dust.

In the meantime the sick man died. His oldest wife who had sat with him, left the hut as he was dying, and went to live with one of his younger wives whose hut was further up the hill. There had been hardly enough vaccine for the natives, and we had not vaccinated ourselves. Trusting to luck with increasing fatalism, however, we awaited the doctor's arrival, preferring to be vaccinated by him. Pouring a tin of paraffin over the dead man's hut, we cremated the corpse, thus evoking some native superstition. What it was they did not tell us, but they regarded us with awe and secret admiration.

It was on the third day after the vaccination when the natives' arms began to swell, that a strange native arrived, saying that the doctor's car had stuck in the mud some eight miles south, and could we send a team of oxen to haul it out. Impatient at three hours' delay, the doctor arrived feeling very irritable.

"Why the Government cannot make a road down this way I don't know," he said, as his car came to a standstill. "Heaven only knows how I shall get back ! "

He was a middle-aged man, very thin and nervy. He had not, he told us, been home to England for fifteen years, but at frequent intervals he sent his family home. His wife was in England now, having an operation. " I wouldn't have her operated on in this country for anything."

After lunch he vaccinated the three of us. John and Marie did not " take," but my arm " took " much more than its share, and did not heal up for several months ! The natives, who lined up with their bandages soiled and out of position—most of them feeling exceedingly sorry for themselves because they were unable to enjoy their holiday—were considered by the doctor to be very satisfactory. After washing his hands in my room, he looked up to the rafters and asked : " You sleep in here ? . . . h'm . . . it isn't exactly a health resort."

Considering how the natives had reacted to the vaccine, I contended that they could not have been immune ; yet there was not a single further case of smallpox in the valley.

# XVI

THE TIME HAD COME FOR JOHN TO RAISE AN overdraft. We needed more oxen, we also needed another cow or two for we were ever short of milk. Early one morning at dawn John rode to Nymba to see the bank manager ; he also went to call on a young farmer " who was doing remarkably well with pigs." At least, so his mother had told our people at home.

Marie was feverish, and was now showing signs of dysentery. My usual splendid standby, *Chavasse's Advice to a Mother*, was not much use to me when it came to tropical diseases. It was unbearably hot in the bedroom where the child, whimpering and crying for water, lay. I was feeling weary and depressed. What was the fundamental reason, I asked myself in moods like these, of being in this particular predicament ? I had almost forgotten. Indeed, I was not certain now. " The search for freedom " and " an open-air life " were mere pious expressions. Neither of them worth having under the circumstances. The chief reason, I expect, for our search after freedom was, perhaps, in order to make money. We wanted, too, as the advertisement said, " Scope for our creative ability." It was to be a " wholesome life " according to some flowery description elsewhere.

John was certainly filled with the urge to create ; he created for all he was worth, but so far it had been anything but wholesome. He had lost a stone in weight and barely touched his food, yet true pioneer that he was, he still seemed happy. The cook sang at the back of the house, his mood at the moment was different from mine. . . . The fellow was sitting on an upturned box, washing his enormous flat feet in the stream. A few minutes later I espied him holding up a small pocket-mirror and making frantic efforts to remove some hair from his chin with a piece of broken bottle ! Presently I heard some heavy footsteps approaching from the store-house. A White man was loitering up the footpath by the stream ; a huge man over six feet high, curly-haired and good-looking in a coarse sort of way. He wore the usual khaki clothes, but round his neck he had a magnificent red silk handkerchief. He pushed his felt hat to the back of his head as he came on to the verandah, asking if John was in. Without being invited, he sat himself down in the one and only comfortable chair.

"My name is Brown," he announced.

Could he, he asked with a jolly grin, have a drink ? There was the unmistakable sign of the drunken blackguard on his handsome face. As I called out to the cook to make a cup of tea the stranger said with a flourish : "If it is all the same to you, dear lady, I'd rather have a spot of whisky." He had, he added, a touch of malaria and whisky was the only thing to check it. Hesitantly I fetched the bottle from the sideboard as well as some water from the filter. With that I let him help himself while I went back to the child who was forever needing my attention. Returning a little later, I saw that the amazing fellow had already consumed a good fourth of the bottle, six shillings' worth to be exact. Presently, after two more drinks, he said :

"So your husband is not here ? When will he be

back ? " Unthinkingly I replied that I expected John back the following afternoon.

I then picked up the bottle and carried it back to the sideboard, leaving the stranger by himself on the verandah. He stretched out his legs, threw his hat on the floor and a fixed stare came into his callous eyes. He then took his gun from the table, eyed it lovingly and said with a sideways glance at me :

" You know, a man is thirsty after tramping twenty miles on an empty stomach." Unwilling to be in his company I left him.

" If you will excuse me while I attend to baby," I said. " I will ask the cook to bring you some food."

The man did not seem to hear me, nor did he seem to notice my apparent coolness. " Lady," he said playfully, pointing his gun towards me, " if you don't mind, I'll have some more of that whisky."

" Don't you think," I asked feeling rather frightened, " that you have had enough ? "

He never took his eyes off me. " I'll tell you when I've had enough," he said, placing the gun across his knee.

The cook took out a plate of bread and cheese on to the verandah while I went back to my bedroom, wondering what to do. What could one do in such a case ? Out of John's drawer I took an automatic revolver and put it in my pocket.

" Bring me that whisky ! " The stranger, who was now lolling back in the chair eyeing his boots, shouted out to the cook.

It so happened that a native policeman was on his weekly rounds, and was at this moment squatting as usual in the kitchen jabbering with the cook. Going to the back, still undecided what to do, I asked him to remain until the White man had gone. " The White man is mad," I said in my faulty Swahili,

" he is full of drink." The policeman did not seem to understand. The infallibility of White people is almost sacred within the simple minds of the natives. The cook, however, understood the situation and explained it to the fellow, who however even then did not seem interested. None of the boys knew who the White stranger was, nor indeed had any of them ever seen him before. Terribly troubled, I returned to the front of the house. The sun was setting and it was time for him to go.

The whisky bottle was now empty. With an ugly grin, the man pointed to the bottle and demanded more.

" I am sorry," I said, " it was all I had ; besides, I must ask you to go, for it will be dark very soon."

" You want me to go ? " he sneered, " and you don't want me to have any more to drink. . . . Well . . ." he rose from the chair, " I'll damn well go when I like, and I'll damn well have some more whisky, do you hear ? " He then picked up his gun and facing me, fired it above my head. The man was terribly drunk, yet he must have been sufficiently sure of himself to avoid hitting me, for I reckon he did not really want to kill me.

Mad with frustration he then went into the room and opened the sideboard. It was empty. Following him, I fingered my revolver, debating with myself whether or not to shoot him. Visions of having to go to court, of living the rest of my life with the thought that I had shot a man, and worst of all, of not being believed in court—crowded through my mind. It was the last thought which stopped me from pressing the trigger. The stranger now began to follow me wherever I went, always aiming his gun at me. Walking to the back of the house to be near the servants, he followed me there. The sight of the black policeman infuriated him, and he fired several shots over the fellow's head. The latter fled as fast as he could, leaving his fez, his gun and puttees, which he had temporarily removed, behind on the kitchen floor.

The cook, that faithful, ugly Kavirondo whose memory I shall bless as long as I live, then ran into my bedroom to fetch John's shotgun. Having loaded it, he came to where I was still dodging the madman. The White man had in the meantime fired his gun in all directions, thus chasing the natives away from their huts so that there was not a soul left near the house—for a native who will bravely face a charging animal, will not stand up to a gun.

Suddenly there was a loud report behind me. Then to my utter amazement the White man started to run. . . . He had been shot in the back ; his legs, though well covered with puttees, were riddled with shots.

It had all been so easy in the end. The cook grinned, his ugly toothless grin ; he had enjoyed the incident enormously.

" *Memsahib*," he said, " this White man very drunk, drunk man, bad man. Sober man, good man. I sleep on doorstep to-night, with gun, good gun."

The houseboy and the cook, as well as half a dozen *shamba* boys armed with spades and pitchforks slept on the verandah outside my door that night. Once it was dark they were not scared. In the dark one man was as good as another, even without a gun. I woke up in the night, shrieking. The experience had had a terrible effect on my already overwrought nerves. I felt years older after this incident.

Two days later a native brought me a letter. It was from the White stranger's wife. " I think it was most careless of you," she wrote, " to give my husband so much to drink. He threatened to kill me when he came home and locked me out for the rest of the night. Please do not think too badly of him," she added, making excuses for him, " he is as good as gold when he is sober." Greatly to my peace of mind, the fellow left the valley almost immediately after my unpleasant experience, having been given the sack.

Since John had been to see the son of his mother's acquaintance, he was thinking of selling his pigs for he was afraid to keep them, fearing their loss through swine-fever. The first thing that the young Etonian did when John arrived was to try to sell him his farm ! John found him all alone without a single thing to do. His farm was not much good ; for one thing it was too close to a crater and his soil was poor. There was no water either, except a couple of tiny hot springs—just a trickle like a leaking tap. The sort of water-supply which might go on for ever or else suddenly cease altogether. He had invested all his capital in pigs, doing quite nicely at first ; indeed, they had thrived and had been sold to the local bacon-factory. But tragedy overtook him. He had had five hundred pigs and lost them all—almost overnight. They did not know at home, not yet.

" I came here," the young man said, " against all the good advice of my family."

He called his farm " Hotair," for the young farmer explained hot air rose from the ground as from a safety-valve and " hot air " had made him come out to Kenya !

" I haven't met anybody yet," said John to me later, " in this blessed paradise who didn't want to sell his farm to me. It makes one think. . . . Well, I'm going to get rid of my pigs though, before they die on my hands."

On the whole I think that we lived too far away from the railway to make pigs a profitable proposition. And the very day before we sold our stock, we had lost our prize boar. A very young boar which we had kept in case of emergency suddenly decided that he was now grown up and past being chivvied about, so he suddenly turned upon the *toto* and chased him furiously. Kariocki just managed to save himself by jumping on to the nearby wagon. The animal then turned and attacked the old boar which had lorded it for so long, and which, taken completely by surprise, was cut about the neck so savagely that he had to be killed.

Eventually a pig-dealer arrived by buggy from a distance of twenty-five miles, to have a look at our " fat stock." But our " fat stock," we found to our dismay, could not be located. Considering that we had at this time about sixty pigs, it seemed incredible that they should be so difficult to find. The dealer, very fat and middle-aged, had, before he came to Kenya, been a butcher in Manchester. Even he, uncritical as he was, found himself yearning for this Midland city. He was telling about the last football-match he had witnessed there exactly twenty years ago. " When I have saved enough, I shall go back there and buy a butcher's shop." His mule was grazing outside the front door while we talked of the happy Midlands, when suddenly our prospective buyer shouted : " What's that over there ? "

In the far distance beyond the lake tiny black specks could be seen moving slowly in our direction. The pigs ! . . . Little did they guess their fate when eventually they were inspected. The ex-butcher did not think much of them and I quite expected him to refuse them. Our delight can be imagined when he took out his cheque book and paid us almost the usual price. The boar was not wanted, so we decided to keep him, as well as one of the sows. After all, they might be useful—if only for food.

Our four new oxen arrived next day and were now being trained. Untrained oxen were much cheaper to buy, but in the long run they didn't pay ; yet economy is an everlasting temptation when one lives on an overdraft ! However, six natives hung on to the raw hide reins which were attached to the yoke on the oxen's neck whilst an enormous tree-trunk was fastened to the animal as well. At first the beast lay down, sulking. It was coaxed for some time and then had its tail twisted. Growing wild, it suddenly rose and turned upon the natives who fairly flew in all directions. The tree trunk seemed to have no weight at all. The infuriated beast heaved and sweated and frothing at the mouth tore wildly down the *shamba*, sweeping aside everything in its way. The natives fell and were dragged along, the bullock fell and rose again, in a regular tornado of dust. Like a battering ram, it struck the ground with one of its horns, breaking it at the root. Then it lay ominously still ; and there it lay until it died, two days later. This was another severe blow to us—and losses like these were becoming monotonous.

Monotonous, too, were the days I spent in bed. . . . Lying in the semi-darkness of the room, listening to the sounds without, watching dark shadows moving through the rafters above, I dreamt of home. . . . I imagined myself somewhere by the cool North Sea, tucked away in the dunes, watching the glorious cloud-formations, walking on the fresh cool sand and following the flight of the gulls. I dreamt that I heard the song of a thrush, that the warbling of a blackbird was sounding in my ear.

Remembering how sorry I used to feel for those

poor mortals who, once a year, exposed their white bodies to the sun—the bank-holiday crowd playing at being free ; how I envied them now ! They were indeed free ; it was I who was in prison. My conception of freedom, I suddenly realised, had completely changed. I remembered, too, the suburban husbands coming home in the cool of the evening to mow their lawns, to cut their hedges—how sorry I once had been for them. Yet how enviable their existence seemed to me now. . . . A praying mantis, which had settled on my bedroom curtain, whistled shrilly. This comical, female insect was singing its hideous love song. Having presently achieved its desire, it cooly devoured its mate, all but the legs, which were apparently too tough. Callously it whistled again for the next victim, which was amazingly soon at hand. . . .

My illness, too, came to an end at last. Weak and ill though I was, I could find no peace in bed. There was the child continually crawling off the verandah without her hat, there was the possibility of her meeting a snake or being molested by the natives, whose idea of amusement was at times more primitive than a monkey's.

# XVII

IT IS DIFFICULT, IF NOT IMPOSSIBLE, FOR ME TO convey on paper the extreme monotony of months and months of drought, when the dust rises high above the trees and nothing of interest really happens. How lifeless the tropics really are, in spite of the hidden life in the bush, the soulless garish birds, an occasional terrifying bush-fire and an abundant insect-life. It knows no song, it has no colour, no scent—and no heart. The White man, be he sensitive, will sooner or later withdraw within himself, become a recluse or take to drink. It is to him an empty world, from which he can get no response.

It is equally difficult to convey the joy and the excitement that the unexpected visit of a White man can cause! In our case, it was almost unbearably exciting, and happened on the average perhaps once a year, not more. It first occurred at the end of our second year. . . . I had just washed my hair and was sitting on the verandah drying it, when there came a sound of many voices from the distance.

A troop of negro-carriers arrived, laden with the usual loads of a safari. The man in front, an enormous Kavirondo, balanced some object on his head which shone brilliantly in the sun. It was a bath, a painted white bath, almost full-size. Behind him walked a native policeman and then followed, one behind the other, about thirty carriers in various stages of un-dress. At the very end of this procession, on a white mule followed our bachelor snob from Nymba—in other words, Freddie. Freddie was the man who had once, now so long ago, sent me those violets ; the man who never went out without a top-hat when in London and who only wore pure silk next to his skin. Freddie, who always carried a silver teapot with him, and who now advertised his coming with a bath, a magnificent affair, weighing about 100 lbs. !

Dismounting from his spotless mule, in a spotless Tussore shirt and corduroy shorts of magnificent fit, Freddie shook hands with me. Freddie was not sensitive, the " rich full warbling of a blackbird," for example, meant precisely nothing to him. He was, though, the right man for his job. About twenty-five men—rather a crowd I thought for the needs of one man, congregated on the grass patch in front of the house and with a shameless groan of relief the carriers flung down their loads, bath and all, and like a pack of thirsty hounds threw themselves down by the stream, burying their faces in the water.

A second policeman arrived in the rear, saluted, stood at attention and politely notified Freddie that two carriers had deserted, having left their loads lying on the roadside. Freddie, who had collapsed in my camp chair, wiped his brow with a white silk handkerchief, ordered his two lanky bobbies to go and bring the deserters back.

" Surely," I said, " they won't find them now ? "

" They'll bring them back all right," answered Freddie supremely confident.

It seemed to have been altogether too easy, for shortly afterwards the two runaways arrived hand-cuffed and very frightened. Having thus captured his brothers, the Askari appeared rather proud of himself and assumed an expression of extreme haughtiness, having at that moment a slight resemblance to a giraffe.

" Smart work," declared Freddie.

The Askari looking even more like a giraffe, then relaxed and sat down on the grass. But why the deserters could not have hidden until nightfall I could not understand ; they were caught on the highway, naïvely having a nap in the midday heat ! Now they stood facing Freddie, looking scared—or sulky as Freddie would have called it. He was now in his element. Still sitting on my chair he was doling out their punishment. Young and immature though he was, he was the Law. He commanded that their trousers—in reality their tattered shorts—be removed, and that each should be given six lashes with a whip. The older of the Askaris unhitched his gun, spat in his hand and then gave a few preliminary cracks with his whip. He did not, however, seem very keen to do his duty, for one of the carriers belonged to his own tribe, and tribesmen are loyal to each other.

It was not violets this time that Freddie brought me. He was going to show me his powers as an administrator of justice instead. In vain I pleaded with him to let the wretched fellows go ; I pleaded until I grew annoyed, and told him to do his Nero-act elsewhere.

" You don't understand," he said, when I returned from my room where I had hidden unwilling to witness the administration of justice, " discipline is good for them. They are like children ; they don't respect a gentle master. The only kind of punishment they really understand is corporal."

" It's strange," I retorted, " that John has never yet had any need to resort to corporal punishment ! "

Freddie did not even bother to reply. There was, of course, no comparison between his position and that of a mere farmer. Besides, no one ever deserted us. . . .

Freddie had come on business, to collect the annual hut-tax from the natives. How they hated digging up their money, which they had secretly buried. Many of them sent their money home to their reserves at frequent intervals, and I have known them to dig up a whole year's wages to give it to a passing tribesman who was on his way to their native village, although they barely knew the fellow. Although the natives never properly understood the meaning of this tax, which to many of them must have seemed like robbery, they never questioned the reason or the right on the part of Freddie to claim it. Besides, there were two policemen there ; that was enough. It was the Law, always a puzzling business, but then the White man, they thought, knew best. The tax was their contribution towards the general administration of the country.

Chaps like Freddie, badly-paid though they were, could not be left to starve. So we had tea on the verandah, silver teapot and all, Freddie sitting on the camp-chair whilst John and I were in a couple of bentwood chairs which we had taken from the dining-room. Suddenly Freddie said : " I don't mind roughing it a bit, you know, now and then." Gravely he contemplated our humble home and found it wanting. " No bathroom ? " he asked. " Which reminds me," he laughed, " that when I was at the Abyssinian border two years ago, I was obliged to take a dozen or so women prisoners. The Askari locked them up in a hut for the night, but, by jove, I couldn't stand it. I had to shift my tent ; the hut, you see, was far too close to me.

Next day I had them taken to the river to be bathed."

Whilst I was trying to locate the houseboy in order to get him to prepare a bath for Freddie before dinner, I found the kitchen completely crowded with carriers and policemen and other tribal friends who were all acting as food tasters. The two deserters, finding it difficult to sit after their recent chastisement, were lying on their stomachs outside the cook's hut, arguing at the top of their voices with the two policemen who, now that they were off duty, had gone very much native again. I threw them each a piece of cake and was rewarded with two cheerful grins. The boys did not seem to bear a grudge against their fate. As Freddie said, they knew that they had deserved it.

In the middle of dinner, which our guest ate in evening dress and John in an ancient pair of tennis trousers, I noticed Freddie suddenly turn very green. He was, too, unusually silent. Eventually, without a word, he left the table. After dinner while John was doing his accounts (entering his losses I expect), Freddie called for me. He lay tossing on the creaky bed as if it had been he who had been whipped. "It's colic," he explained. He had it periodically and the only thing that relieved the attack was a dose of castor oil with a dash of brandy in it. Alas, I had no brandy, but there was plenty of oil in the house. As I went into the kitchen to find it the natives skiddaddled like mice. They had been eating the rest of our joint, and now each had a cup of tea poured from my silver teapot.

" The *Bwana* very ill inside his stomach," said the cook. "Ah," he shook his head sagely, " it is bad to flog boys, very bad,"—a remark which suggested that through some occult power Africa was revenging herself on Freddie. I had never enjoyed giving anyone a dose of castor oil, but dosing Freddie was another matter !

He was all right again next day, when there was another minor matter which needed attention. Two men wanted a " palaver " with him about a woman. They wanted to know about the White man's law. One of the fellows said that the woman was his as she had lived with him for many years, although he confessed that he had never been married to her. The other argued that the woman now wanted to live with him as she had grown tired of her mate. The woman sat sobbing on a tree stump, rubbing an enormous bump on her head which had been administered by her first lover. She wanted to leave him badly, she told Freddie.

"Well," declared he, "the White man's law says that the woman is free to do as she likes, as she is not married. But you," Freddie shouted to the first chap, "must marry her at once ; if not, then you" he pointed to the other suitor " must marry her."

" Marry her ? " the first cried.

" Marry her ? " the second repeated.

It was evident that they did not like the White man's law. Keep her, yes, but not marry her. She was, when all was said and done, very much second-hand. Didn't Freddie think so, too ? The two lovers looked as though they were going to have it out between them but John would have none of that. Freddie sent the woman home to her father's hut, some eighty miles away. She went—alone. Neither of her lovers followed her. Socially she was now an outcast. Her father might even refuse to take her in ; probably he would have to sell her cheap, or perhaps exchange her for a goat.

After our midday meal, Freddie went his way,

returning to Nymba.  His visit had been an interlude, and as such a pleasant change.  The enamel bath had not been used, for the houseboy had mistakenly given him mine which was of the ordinary galvanised variety. . . .

# XVIII

THE OXEN WERE TAKEN FROM THE PLOUGH ONCE more to go on the weariest journey imaginable. The Masai walked ahead, his sphinx-like face completely expressionless. Marie had been stricken with an eye disease which I did not understand ; her eyelids had swelled up dreadfully. The carrier who had been to tell the doctor had returned with a bottle of nitrate of silver and some hazy instructions about putting a drop or two into the corner of the child's eyes. He did not tell me that the intensely swollen and painful eyelids had to be forced open. Marie grew steadily worse, and eventually there was nothing else to do but to take her in to Nymba. From dawn, through the heat of the day, we drove up the Simba valley at a steady two-and-a-half to three miles an hour. The road was heavy with red dust and the farms we passed at rare intervals were looking dry and deserted. I had passed this way before—on my journey of discovery, but it was not so interesting now. I was only conscious of an almost unbearable strain, trying to shade the burning sun from the sick baby with an umbrella and being jolted on a springless bullock-cart for twelve solid hours.

The cook, who in common with all natives took tragedy for granted, said : " The *toto* (baby) will be blind, completely blind. All the babies with this illness are blind afterwards." On this, my way to Calvary, I felt profoundly critical of the whole of my existence, as well as my surroundings. It seemed a dead, unreal world. The driver cursed and spat, the leader yawned incessantly. Plodding on and on like this, to the accompaniment of a squeaking wagon, is an experience which has an indescribably depressing effect on anyone but a negro. The oxen shuffled along clumsily, their heads hanging down, too exhausted to snatch even a mouthful of grass from the ground, as they did earlier in the morning when travel seemed still pleasant.

There is no magic in the middle of the day in Africa. A few white butterflies hovered in the still air ; that was all. At noon Kenya leaves you alone to your own devices ; like a sleeping cat, it awakes and stretches itself at sunset. A couple of gazelles crossed our path ; some vultures dropped from the sky, skimmed above us curiously and then flew off again. We had not met a single soul, white or black. Facing the dying sun at last, we had for the first time to apply the brakes. Below us, in a kind of dream, lay Nymba. Zigzagging down, we met a cloud of sandflies which covered our hands and faces and clung to our hair and stung.

Luckily, almost the first house on the outskirts was the hospital. The Masai stopped the team and promptly sat down in the dust. Sick-looking negroes crept about the littered compound ; immediately behind their sleeping-quarters loomed the local church-yard. " Dead and alive, dead and alive," the rhythm of the bullock-cart had seemed to say as it had rumbled along. "Dead and alive," I now repeated to myself. It was silly thus to repeat, but it seemed to express the whole atmosphere of the situation.

Gravely the doctor examined the infant, trying to open her swollen eyelids ; but Marie, who had been almost lifeless in my arms all through the day, began to struggle and scream. Slightly annoyed, he went to fetch his Indian assistant, who also examined the child, apparently with a better knowledge of this particular disease. His hands were calmer, steadier, than those of the fever-stricken White man. It was the Indian who now seemed to take the professional lead in the case ; it was he who had a calming effect upon the child and myself. He called out for two native nurses who, dressed in white overalls, came hurrying in. They held the baby's legs and head whilst the Indian doctor lifted the swoolen eyelids and quickly dropped some liquid directly into the infant's eyes. What a different process from my futile attempt back on the farm ! The Indian showed me a white spot which had developed on one of Marie's eyes, a thickening of the conjunctiva.

" It is good that you have come ; soon it would have been blind, this eye. The child," he added, looking at me rather searchingly, " will be all right. But it is you, lady, if I may suggest it, who needs a change of air."

He smiled. It was, he knew, futile to suggest sending people home if they had only comparatively recently arrived in Africa to make a new home for themselves. After all, their idea usually was to stay, to enjoy the " glorious climate," not to flee from it. Besides, he knew that funds were not so easily come by to go home with, unless of course you were a Government official. The doctor had had a great deal of experience with White people on the equator, he said. . . .

It was now dark and Nymba had come to life. The Masai was asleep beneath the hoofs of the oxen and the driver was gambling with some heavily-bandaged native patients by the hospital gates. They played a kind of " Put and Take " with white stones. I noticed that our driver lost several cents. Slowly we drove through the main streets. Two other wagons, filled with stores, passed us on the outward journey, travelling through the night for preference.

A white-haired negro clerk locked up the tiny court-house and lit his pipe. The majority of the White inhabitants (who had probably spent the afternoon at home asleep) were sitting on the club-house verandah and in the hotel bar. To crown a really scorching day, they needed the one and only stimulant available—a drink. The manager of Nymba's Grand Hotel, who was very pleased to see me once more, looked distinctly overdressed in a navy blue suit of pre-war cut. He was on his way to a Masonic Meeting. There were about four Free-masons in the whole of Nymba, and the " Hall " was down by the lake.

" You wouldn't notice it," said the manager, " it's only a hut built of straw. . . . But you don't look very grand," he added, holding up the kerosene-lamp to my face.

He was in a hurry, but showed us to our room before he left. Jeyes' fluid, I noticed, still filled the air, conjuring up past memories.

The child was thirsty so the first iob I set myself was to boil some water, for there was no milk to be had. Indeed, there was always this shortage of milk wherever one went in Kenya. Single-handed, I then treated the child's eyes once more, after which I went to bed. . . . Lying upon my back, I re-lived the hours which I had spent in the self-same room. Since those far-off days, life had been far from idyllic. I heard the Masai drive the oxen past the window ; the midnight train arrived from

Nairobi, whistling shrilly ; on a seat beneath my window a White woman was being made love to by a White man—not her husband. . . .

How black the night seemed to me—but there was a lovely dawn in store. For the first time for a fortnight, little Marie smiled again, and opened her eyes as far as she could. Life, I felt, was worth living again ! What did it matter if, when looking into the mirror, I saw my own eyelids swollen and discharging ? I now knew how to check the inflammation.

We returned to Simba two days later, laden with such luxuries as a bag of South African tobacco for John, a bundle of magazines nearly two months old, some lengths of mosquito netting, new tooth brushes, another bottle of whisky. But I'm afraid—speaking of myself—that both my eyes were nearly closed. . . .

## XIX

IT WAS THE BEGINNING OF OUR THIRD YEAR ON the farm when the rains came with a vengeance. I was alone, waiting for John to return. He had again gone to buy yet another cow—a necessity but a doubtful investment. It was dark and the natives in their compound were asleep. John had never been so late before. I sat and listened ; I tried to read, but the lamp burned low and then went out. Big drops of rain fell on the roof—seemed as if the heavens had been let loose. I sat listening to the thundering downpour in the dark for a long time ; then I decided to go to bed.

Placing my feet to the ground I noticed to my horror that I stood in water. There was a pool in the centre of the room four inches deep, and still the water came creeping in from behind the door. I did not care. Extraordinary, I reflected, how one ceases to care about almost anything. Picking up my books out of a puddle, I waded to bed ; and for companionship took Marie from the cot and laid her down beside me. Still I listened for John's return. . . . Presently a faint sound came from the back-door, which I knew was locked. Perhaps, thought I, it is the water encroaching still further into the house.

With trembling hands I lit the candle and, peering over the edge of the bed, I saw something creeping by the door. It was a snake, a black mamba which was seeking shelter from the rain. Gliding daintily

116

on to a chair to avoid the wet, its eyes shone like diamonds in the light of the candle. There was, I realised, nothing that I could do except shout, but that, I knew, would be useless for none would hear me. I tucked the mosquito-netting tightly around the mattress and prepared to share the room for the night with one of the deadliest snakes of Africa. I now realised that John would not return that night, and overcome with the fatigue of waiting, I at last fell asleep. At dawn the snake had gone, as mysteriously as it had come. . . .

John returned early the following morning and straightway began to sow. My experience with the mamba faded into insignificance, for now the time had arrived for thrilling activity. Visions of splendid crops of maize and ultimate success spurred him on to work from dawn till sunset. It would be, he reckoned, three more years before the coffee-trees would bear. In the meantime maize was the important thing, for nothing but maize would keep us going. Mud-caked oxen tugged at the plough, swishing their tails to keep off the mosquitoes, while John walked knee-deep in the mud.

With amazing rapidity the first green shoots of maize appeared above the ground. But there was an unpleasant dampness everywhere about the house : the floors and beds were damp ; everything began to rust and even my groceries grew mildewed. The wind and the rain raged for several hours every day—veritable tempests of thunder and lightning and hail. The wind whistled through the corrugated-iron roof, driving the water into the cracks ; water dripped from the rafters on to the beds and tables. Our one fear was that we should now be blessed with too much rain.

John sat on the couch during the evenings, his hands

hanging in front of him, tired out. Too tired to read, too tired to think. . . . He hadn't written home for ages. What, after all, was there to tell? He was not the sort to describe his hardships or mention his fears and discomforts. I turned on the gramophone again and again. The "Barcarole" reeled off slightly more scratchy now, invariably dropping to a lower key at the end of the record. Time for meditation. Meditation, however, that was not very pleasant. . . . There was too much water everywhere. It lay about in pools and in every conceivable place anopheles were hatching their eggs. It seemed at this moment a dead certainty that the crop would again be ruined. Ever since we had been here, John had been in constant conflict with the elements. Kenya was untamable. It yielded at times, but unwillingly ; blessing with a good crop the labour of years, yet snatching back again what had so painfully been wrested from it.

We were both exceedingly pleased when cousin Jim arrived for a fortnight's holiday. Things, we felt, were easier to bear in the company of others. Poor cousin Jim, he did not quite know what he was in for ! Never before had he come into close contact with unadulterated pioneering, and it was clear to us that the experience shocked him. It was populous where Jim came from, within a few miles of Nairobi. Compared to Simba, life was civilised. . . . He belonged to a tennis-club and was captain of a football team, and I think that he even played polo occasionally. In short, Jim had never experienced difficulties such as daily confronted us. To him transport difficulties were non-existent, the ever-threatening disappointments with crops and the ravages of droughts did not affect his own pocket. His salary was secure.

He had, too, in the face of hostile Africa, been able
to retain that exalted " Empire Builder " attitude
inherited from his father, and still spoke glowingly
of " adventure " and the glories of the " open spaces ";
of doing something " worth-while," and of being
one of the world's producers. How he persistently
deluded himself, I do not know. Yet in a way it was
a blessing. Jim's job was simple enough, his boss was
rich ; and there were on his farm several tractors
driven by well-trained natives. From all accounts his
daily routine was to blow a whistle at 7 a.m., tell the
foreman what to do (and see that his orders were
carried out), and spend the rest of the day reading
detective yarns ! There was even a river not too far
away, where he " got some jolly fine fishing." But
now, he said, he was getting a bit fed up with being
the only bachelor amongst his pals. As a matter of
fact, he had recently met a girl who had come out to
Kenya as a governess and had seriously thought of
asking her to marry him. . . .

Taking a photograph from his pocket-case he pointed
out the girl to me. I could hardly repress a smile,
for if ever a girl looked a governess, this girl did !
She wore an outsize pair of horn-rimmed glasses,
her chest was flat and her lack of figure so directly
opposite to Jim's former idea of what a woman
should look like, that I did not know what to say.
That this little wallflower of a girl should appeal to
Jim seemed unbelievable ; but I was fully aware
that isolation and lack of choice led many a young
man in the colonies to marry a girl quite opposite
to his previous conception of woman. Had Jim, for
instance, met this girl in England, he would never
have looked at her twice.

" Nice life this ! " burst out cousin Jim as he lit
his fiftieth cigarette that day. His feet were on the

verandah fence whilst the rest of his body was drowned in my camp-chair, which had begun to sag badly lately. " So free," he went on, " a chap can do just what he likes ! "

" Free for what ? " I asked, thinking of John wading in the mud at the far end of the farm.

" Well," he hesitated, " just free, that's all. A chap can jolly well do as he likes here ; you need not dress," Jim paused to scratch himself for the fleas of the whole neighbourhood had fled to the house since the rains had come. " You can let your beard grow," he went on, counting his blessings. " You can get drunk if you like ; you need not go to church either," he added lamely, suddenly remembering that even at home he never went to church. " You needn't be a Rotarian or belong to the Chamber of Commerce against your will, or any other rotten sort of institution."

" It doesn't seem free to me, Jim," I ventured. " On the contrary, we are tied hand and foot here. I don't have to dress I know, but then I never minded dressing. Dressing is fun, Jim ; I miss it. You have to have your bath every night, more so than at home, and it takes I reckon a good half-hour to remove the fleas and ticks which have collected in your clothes and on your body. I spend a good ten minutes every night looking for jiggers and removing them carefully from underneath my toe-nails. I frequently wash my hair, and have to cut John's as well as Marie's. Ah, I would give a lot to have that bath we had in the old home at Mannington, minus paint as it was."

Jim lit another cigarette. " Ah," he exulted, " give me the open spaces ; besides, no one cares a damn what you do ! "

No one cared much, I knew, yet nevertheless

everyone certainly knew what one did. The natives knew everything, they gossiped with gusto. If a man in a neighbouring valley, fifty miles away, experimented with a crop of flax or a batch of tobacco, we heard about it. If he drank, we knew ; if he failed, the whole country knew ; and if he secretly owned a *bibi* (native woman) we also knew. We heard of floggings committed seventy miles away and of *memsahibs* who were fond of other *bwanas* apart from their own. There is nothing so interesting, so absorbing to the natives as the love-life of the White man. The servants discussed Jim for hours, speculating as to his relationship to me. Was he lover or brother ; and if not, why not?

As we always turned in early because there was absolutely nothing else to do once darkness had fallen except read (if there was anything to read) and write letters, Jim grew pretty restless. Sitting on the verandah was hopeless after dark because of the mosquitoes. Indoors it was better if you closed the doors. We smoked, played dominoes, and Jim showed me some card tricks. We also talked of home. Whether he knew it or not, Jim invariably talked of home when he was tired. . . .

Something interesting and rather rare happened the first night that cousin Jim arrived ; an incident which caused great excitement amongst the natives as well as in Jim's heart. Two elephants had descended from the escarpment which rose to the west, and had walked through our maize which was now almost three feet high, leaving footprints as big as card tables. They crossed by the maize store and went coolly down the main road to the saltlick by the lake. No one had either seen or heard them.

" Imagine, just imagine," said Jim, " that about one hundred and fifty pounds worth of ivory were

parading past your house ! " He sighed. " I'm
blowed if I'm going to bed to-night."

" You've got to have a licence, Jim, before you can
shoot elephants."

" There's time enough to send for a licence when
I bag one. Besides, don't you see, they're damaging
your crop."

Fondly imagining that the two beasts would return,
Jim built himself a seat on the roof of the storehouse,
which adjoined the maize field. He was going to sit
up for them ; rain or no rain, he did not care. Feeling
cheerful and filled with pleasant boyish anticipation,
Jim went roaming about with his well-cleaned guns
and returned at tea-time with a wart-hog, a water-
buck and a couple of guinea-fowl. He had set out
for the fun of the thing, not for necessity. Indeed,
had he come across a kongoni and a couple of elands,
he would have shot them, too. That's what they were
for, just sport !

" Who is going to eat all this meat ? " I asked.

" Good lord," replied Jim, " who wants to worry
about that ? Look at this lovely pair of horns, and
Joan, look, have you ever seen a better pair of
tusks ? "

Whistling and blissfully happy, Jim scraped off the
flesh from the two heads and then tied them to the
verandah rail to let the sun do the rest. In his opinion,
these trophies were worth keeping. The sun, however,
failed to do the job as rapidly as he had anticipated,
and by tea-time the smell was indescribable, which
attracted every fly in the district ! The flies swarmed
on the food and drowned in the teacups, but the men
did not seem to mind either the smell or the flies. . . .
This was Jim's sense of freedom ; he could not have
indulged in such exciting activities at home !

John having less faith in the return of the elephants,

placidly replanted the trodden-down maize and then went to bed.

"Well, good night, Joan," called out Jim as he went off with a blanket, a mackintosh and a couple of guns to his abode in the snake-infested barn. He came back once more, though ; he had forgotten the ammunition. I lay listening for a long time before I went to sleep. I heard the faint " barking " of distant zebras and the crazy sound of a laughing hyena.

When I awoke at dawn, it was to hear Jim throwing himself on to his creaking bed in the room next to ours, talking angrily to himself.

" Well I'm damned ! " came through the partition.

Something had evidently gone wrong. And it turned out to be the trophies on the verandah-rail. They had gone. A hyena, probably. The elephants, too, had let him down whilst his face was swollen with mosquito-bites. All in all, it had not been worth while. The ants, too, had found him out—high above under the roof. Up they had climbed, thousands of them, a regular pilgrimage of red ants. Jim was stung from head to foot and was finally driven off his perch. . . .

## XX

WE, TOO, WERE TO HAVE A NIGHTMARISH EXPERI-
ence with the repulsive reddish-black and long-legged
ants which bite so viciously and which frequently
leave their heads behind when removed from their
momentary occupation of digging their fangs into the
flesh of their victims.

A night or two after Jim's adventure, these fiendish
insects fairly flooded our bedroom while we were
asleep, swarming into the child's cot. Luckily she
awoke and called out before they had bitten her.
Their charming method of torture is not to bite until
the victim is covered from head to foot. And then—
at a given signal from the leader, they attack simultaneously. It was in this way that they killed chickens
and goats and other helpless things.

Picking up the child from the cot, I felt almost sick
with shock. Little Marie's head was swarming with
the ants ! Grabbing a bottle of Lysol, I poured most
of the contents over her hair while John fetched
buckets of boiling water from the boiler in the back-
yard, and poured it over the floor in all directions.
By now I was being stung to distraction by the angry
little beasts. The beds, too, were swarming with
them. But their well-ordered campaign had been
completely upset and they fled in chaos. The cook
awoke and, as was usual in an emergency, was full of
help and advice.

"Those *dudahs*," he said, "are indeed *mbeia sana*

(very bad)." His brother had lost a child through ants. The child was dead in the morning, completely eaten away, just a bone left, nothing else. *Kufa kafiza* it was, completely dead. This was the second *toto* his brother had lost. Considering that his brother was a Christian—had, in fact, become a Christian to please the White man, it had not been very considerate of the White man's god. Considering, too, that his Christian brother, like himself, was having, according to his faith, only one miserable wife, this wholesale loss of children was a serious matter for him. The second *toto*, he added with a chuckle, had not had such an unpleasant death as the first one; at least he did not think so. He had merely been stolen by a hawk, when just a fortnight old. His mother, it appears, looked up one day from her work in the field and saw him disappear over the distant hill. . . . It was more pleasant, though, to be carried away and to be made an end of by a vulture than to be slowly eaten to death by ants, didn't I think so? The cook looked thoughtful and then suddenly handled the charm that dangled from a chain round his waist. Charms, he hinted, didn't always work—even Catholic ones.

"You have been very lucky," he assured me as he wielded the broom, "that your *toto* isn't dead now."

He then went out on to the rubbish-heap and with the aid of match-light collected all the empty cigarette tins which cousin Jim had thrown away. The fellow placed each leg of the iron bedsteads in a tin, filling each tin with paraffin.

"No *dudah*," he said, "will come up from below. All that you will get now, are those from above."

Sleep did not come easily after our grim experience; but thoughts, unpleasant thoughts, came crowding in on me. I was getting introspective and afraid. . . . The country seemed treacherous and cruel. Jim felt cross and taciturn when he rose at 11 a.m. next morning. He was, he said, itching from head to foot, and one of his eyes was almost closed.

" I'm beginning to think I don't know this damned country as it really is. Every damned thing that crawls or flies seems to sting ! I'm sure that I was stung by a moth last night."

He kicked everything out of his way—even his gun lay neglected, and he didn't even bother to shave.

" Let's kill a pig," he suggested an hour later, still dressed in his pyjamas. " I'd like some pork, I haven't eaten any pork for years . . . besides . . . I want to kill something."

Our one remaining sow having done her duty; we were now again in the happy possession of eight pigs. Almost immediately after, Jim started chasing the pigs. Down the path he went, over the stream and back again, round the shed, until eventually he caught one of the pigs by the tail. He was evidently enjoying himself and the elephants were forgotten. . . . It was later in the afternoon that I found him and the cook kneeling on the verandah beneath my bedroom window, scalding the pig and using my bath tub for the purpose. Jim, thoroughly absorbed, scraped it with vigour, having in turns tried to do it with a knife, a brush and a razor ! The sickly smell of scalded pig, the clinging bristles and the muggy heat did not deter him nor did it spoil his appetite for pork. When the job was finished, Jim tipped up the bath and calmly let the water flow over the verandah. Slowly it trickled into my bedroom, over the steps, spreading bristles everywhere.

The natives came to beg for pork. First the cook, then the houseboy and later on a passing policeman.

Jim was now at a loose end; no company, no elephants and not a single book to read. Well over fifty times he played the " Barcarole." Whilst every two hours or so he bathed in our home-made pool— that is to say, when it was full. Frequently it suddenly emptied itself, as if someone had pulled a plug ! A leakage here and there, and the bather was left high and dry in a bath of mud, and covered with leeches. With youthful patience, Jim banked up the dam with branches, wood and tons of mud, and quickly, before it leaked, he again dived into the muddy pool. He dived well and was greatly admired by the watching natives. Jim sat on the diving-board picking leeches off his body, when Kamau the houseboy asked to be allowed to dive as well. Joyfully he removed his khaki shorts, his crucifix and his *kansa* and with a great deal of swaggering he dived in—feet first ! Amazing though it may sound the boy never rose to the surface again ! A splash, a ripple—and then silence. We waited patiently for a while, expecting him to rise again at any moment, for we had all seen natives dive for pennies, dodging the sharks in the harbour of Mombasa, and had seen them stop under water for incredible lengths of time. The total disappearance of the boy, however, was too much for Jim. He decided to dive for him. As Jim dived into the twelve feet or so of water, the cook, who had been watching the proceedings, told me that he knew—that in fact they all knew that Kamau could not swim.

" No Kikuyu," he said, spitting contemptuously, " can swim." They had egged Kamau on to do as the White man had done.

" Good heavens, don't you see that Kamau might be drowned ? " I cried horrified.

The cook shrugged his shoulders. " That," he said " would be *shauri a mungu* " (God's own affair), and he smiled. "There are many more Kikuyus where Kamau came from."

This was evidently the kind of joke a native understood ! Presently, after what seemed to me a very long time, Jim located the missing boy and appeared on the surface with him slung over his shoulder. Dazed and speechless, as well as choked with water, the Kikuyu lay on the grass struggling for breath. He had had a nasty shock. He thought, naïvely, that all men could swim, but now his enthusiasm for diving had gone. Having coughed up a great deal of water, Kamau dressed and calmly went back to the house to get our tea ready !

Jim, towards the end of his fortnight's holiday, sat about rather listlessly doing nothing at all, except smoke and scratch. I realised that he would soon grow resigned and perhaps deteriorate, if he had to live down our valley. There was no fun, nothing to do at all, apart from going out for buck and other live creatures. That, too, was not much fun if one had to go alone.

"Christ ! " he exclaimed, " if I had to live here for years on end, I should feel as though I were waiting for death to overtake me. For goodness sake let's do something, let's have a *ngoma* (a native dance) on Sunday. I shall die of boredom unless something happens pretty soon," he moaned.

"The open spaces," I observed quietly, " are not so exciting after all."

Jim did not even bother to reply.

Scores of negroes arrived on Sunday afternoon for the *Ngoma*, the popular native entertainment. John had killed an ox which they were going to roast over an open fire. Women, dozens of them startlingly ugly and seemingly all alike, stood in a circle shoulder to shoulder, doing a kind of stationary dance, using

their stomach-muscles and shaking their heads. It
was very hot, and Jim was in low spirits. "Damned
funny," was his only remark all afternoon. The meat
of the ox was tough, but the natives did not seem to
mind. The animal had been long past its prime and
had been dragging sadly behind in the team. After
an hour's dancing, the ground was fairly churned
up into an almost knee-deep slush. Eventually the
real actors, the true performers of the *Ngoma* arrived.
The warriors were magnificently painted though completely naked, except for some gorgeous anklets and
head-dresses made of bead embroidered leather and
ostrich-feathers. The actors leapt into the ring,
preening themselves this way and that, while the
women shrieked and applauded with traditional
admiration. How the young men swaggered, throwing their spears into the air, leaping gracefully from
the ground like Russian ballet-dancers ! Old men
squatted, huddled under the trees, gorging themselves
with meat ; a greedy, senile heap of skin and bones.
The women clapped with wild enthusiasm every time
a warrior entered the ring to have a mock fight with
an imaginary foe. All danced and danced until
almost insane, then they threw themselves upon the
wet grass through sheer exhaustion.

At sunset the women grew slightly more unbalanced,
and one or two of them came dancing and wriggling
up to the foot of our verandah where Jim sat smoking
his pipe, and with gestures, if not with words, showed
him that though he was only white and not really
beautiful to behold, that though he could not wield
a spear, he nevertheless was a man and as far as they
were concerned he, too, was pleasing. Embarrassed,
Jim retired indoors, slamming the door, and then went
to bed. The *Ngoma* at long last came to an end, so
it was now the young people's turn to feast. They ate

incredible quantities of almost raw meant and very soon felt the need for sleep. Many were violently sick. Creeping into their huts like tired dogs, they left the night to its own usual indifference. They had, I know, enjoyed themselves.

Feeling infinitely brighter, Jim left for Nymba the following morning on John's bike. How unbearably monotonous it was going to be after he had gone !

" Sorry, Joan," he said, " I hate to leave you— down here. When I'm married you'll have to come and stay with us and then we'll have a really good time."

Once more he waved his hand in the general direction of the " open spaces " before he disappeared round the bend. He was going to have a difficult journey ahead of him, for the road was sodden and the streams were running high.

# XXI

IN SPITE OF THE ABNORMALLY BIG RAINFALL, WE
had a good crop of maize. It was most stimulating
and once more we mentally made our fortune.
Once more we sat over our books and reckoned up
our present blessings and our future profits. Further,
neither of us had had any malaria for at least four
months ! We should be able, we conjectured, to
wipe out our overdraft and to have nearly enough
left over to last through another year. We needed
new clothes, we also needed the attention of a dentist.
In reality we both needed a change of air ; but next
year, we declared, would do just as well. Our
bullock-cart was doing the journey to Nymba as
often as three times a week to deliver the maize at
the station.

Kamau, the houseboy, had been to Nairobi for a
week and had now lost his old contentment. He
had fallen a victim of so-called civilisation ; had
become utterly fascinated by the advancement of his
old friends who were engaged as cooks and chauffeurs
and who wore clothes " as good," he said, " as
district commissioners." He was restless. His father
had lately come to live with him—a dignified, serene
and completely unadorned old man who sat in the
shade of his hut and, who knows, dreamt of his warlike
past while his son was " caught " and impressed by
the cheapest mass-product of European importation.

The cook, too, was restless in another way ; he was subjected to periodical attacks of religious fervour. Once a month he went to church, which meant going at a steady trot for thirty miles (starting off Saturday evening), arriving at the church-door just in time for early Communion on Sunday morning. Confession and Communion over and feeling thoroughly relieved of his sins, he then went—so he told me—to visit his lady-friends at the bazaar, who always took the money he had on him. Broke and tired, he would arrive back at the farm to cook our breakfast on Monday morning ; setting again to work with a regular frenzy, making pastry and bread and cape gooseberry pie. If any of his confections did not turn out a perfect success, he hid them in a box under the kitchen-table and shared them with his friend, the policeman. He would have gladly fed a regiment ; unexpected visitors did not throw him into a panic. He could make soup out of almost anything ; bits of vegetable, wild spinach and mushrooms were sufficient for a three-course meal. His potato crisp, his bread and his pastry were delicious and worthy of a salary five times that which we could afford to pay him. I often wondered why he stopped with us, considering the wages he could have earned elsewhere. It was perhaps because I never interfered with him. Had I even found fault with him it would have deeply hurt him.

The months ahead of us, after the season of maize-picking was over, were as usual monotonously uneventful.

Women and children had turned out to help ; dusky fingers picking lazily, beginning to know the curse of Adam. John tried to grow a second crop of maize as was sometimes possible if the rains were good. And he almost succeeded, half an acre or so actually

matured. . . . Our banana-trees commenced to bear
fruit in abundance, and we had so much that we
constantly gave it away.  But after a time we heartily
disliked bananas, whilst not even the pigs would
eat them !

A native died of fever.  " The earth," so he said
before he died, " had hit him in the face every time
he tried to raise himself."  No one seemed to mourn
him. He was dead. That was that. The children did
not seem to miss him, nor did his wives.  Death is
not so very vital.  Indeed, if a man is seriously ill, his
family will mercifully hasten his end by carrying him
into the bush so that the hyenas, jackals and vultures
may do the rest.  This method also saves the dead
man's family touching the corpse, which is strictly
*taboo.*  The dead man will then enter heaven, the
Black man's heaven where according to his deserts
he will be given a herd of cattle, or perhaps only a
couple of goats.  The latter would probably be
his hell. . . .

Attached as I was to the natives as well as conscious
of having intruded into their own province, of having
helped to deprive them of some of their freedom, my
pity was all for the plodding White man.  For his
need and his capacity for suffering are infinitely
greater.  Sunday, which might so easily have been
forgotten, was especially observed by all the natives,
Christian and otherwise ;  and John and I, as well
as the baby (who had grown into a thin, rather pale
little girl) often spent Sunday afternoons by the hot
spring which was the source of our stream.  The
stream rippled between enormous trees covered with
fungus which hung like giant ropes to the ground.
The natives called it " stream of snakes."  Silvery
water-snakes wriggled down-stream, almost indis-
tinguishable from the water itself.  Several times we

surprised the natives bathing or washing their blankets in the hot pool, whilst a quarter of a mile further down-stream the cook filled the pitcher with the self-same water for our table! Yet it was perfectly clean. Once only did I feel disinclined to drink.

It was Sunday afternoon, I remember, and all the men were visiting, walking from farm to farm. Being Sunday and in common with European villagers, the natives believed in dressing up, in wearing something which, decorative though it might be, was rarely comfortable. This being the Sabbath day they wore shoes—yellow shoes, white shoes and some of imitation crocodile. Their feet being permitted perfect freedom for six days out of the seven, they invariably felt " the pinch." Some also wore hats and trousers. Anyhow, the cook who was staying at home to watch his wife, came running into tell me that a woman with leprosy was washing her feet in our drinking-pool! He had told her to " *quenda* " (go), but she had only sworn at him and had told him he was the " son of a hundred snakes." He wanted to know if he should " biff her over the head " with his knob-kerry, or was it better to leave her alone, this being Sunday, the day of our Lord and Christian charity? How difficult it was to live the life of a Christian in the eyes of the natives! It may be written against me, but I sent the leper away without the slightest pity.

Mice and rats had multiplied enormously since we had arrived. In the peace of the Sunday afternoons they came from their hiding-places and fairly frolicked in the open. Sitting absolutely still, we watched them having a game of " follow my leader " from the store-room to the kitchen, round the far end of the house and over to the barn. John, with nothing more urgent to do, sat in the camp-chair popping them off with his ·22 as they came round the corner. Sometimes he missed. Occasionally there was a lull in the procession and then the manœuvres started all over again. There were grey mice, black mice and speckled mice. Once a grey snake, some five feet long, was also watching the frolicking and then proceeded to swallow the mice wholesale ! This was easily the most exciting Sunday afternoon we spent in the " back of beyond." We fairly revelled in this " freedom " and John had not even bothered to shave. . . .

A great deal of nonsense has been written about a fellow hearing the irresistible Call of Africa, if he has once lived there. I have yet to meet the man who honestly yearns for a life such as we were living, if he can settle down in a place where the air is cool, where he can work without being defeated. Certainly many do return again, but they would not do so if they had any other choice. From my experience they usually *pretended* to like the life but their enthusiasm seemed to sound a bit hollow. . . .

# XXII

O NE DAY IN THE DRY SEASON WHEN IT WAS AUTUMN
at home, two little birds arrived and built their nest
above our door. To me they looked like swallows :
swiftly-flying birds with graceful, forked tails. Their
arrival heralded a great deal of bustle and excitement
under the roof (I imagined that they had come from
England in search of another summer), and they
built the same kind of nest that I had seen swallows
build at home. In due time and after a great deal
of fuss, the fledglings arrived, four of them. Shortly
after they had been hatched I found another nest
of newly-hatched birds lying on the ground under a
grenadilla bush. They opened their grotesquely large
and hungry mouths as I picked them up and replaced
them in the shade of a branch. I don't know what
kind of birds they were, but they were grey and eager.
Hiding myself under the banana-palms some distance
away I waited for the mother bird to return. She
never came. Below me the second sowing of maize
gently swayed in the haze, and it was so still that even
those most observant animals, the monkeys, did not
notice me.

But I saw them ! They came cautiously, one behind
the other, towards the golden corn, each picking as
many cobs as it could carry. Two baby monkeys
walked ahead of their male parent, who presently
boxed their ears like a human father, for getting in

his way! As soon as I rose from my hiding-place I was immediately spotted by a monkey-spy which sat in a tree bordering the wood. He promptly signalled to the others. A faint whistling brought them to a sudden standstill. Fourteen of their number stood motionless within twenty feet of me. I, too, stood still and then suddenly raising my hand, they dashed helter-skelter into the wood, not one of them dropping a single cob on the way.

Going back to the bush next morning I found the nest still there, and the little birds despairingly hungry. So I decided to take them home. Climbing a ladder, I gently placed the babies in the swallows' nest where there seemed sufficient room for them all. After some time the mother-bird returned and circled round the nest in great excitement. It did not look very promising. Off she went again and I feared she might desert her own family and the little strangers altogether. But she had gone to fetch her mate. Back they came together discussing the matter in a sharp, metallic language. "Eight hungry mouths to feed!" they seemed to say in consternation. Eight hungry mouths yawned greedily as the mother perched on the edge of the nest, while the male bird sat on a branch nearby. She did not feed them, though—not even her own—yet it was obviously long past feeding-time. Away the mother-bird flew again to discuss the matter once more with her mate, and yet again she returned, as if to make sure that what she had said she had seen was not an illusion. "There *are* eight," she seemed to repeat again and again. The male bird, too, came back to count them, after which they disappeared—apparently for good. I climbed the steps and started to feed them myself, dropping wet soft crumbs into their willing mouths.

Shortly before sunset the parents again returned, still excited and indignant. The mother-bird had yet another look at the crowded nest, and for some time I thought she was going to make the best of the new position. I could just see her tail-feathers from below.

After we had had our tea and it was nearly dark, I was shocked to discover four little birds dead lying on the verandah floor. The mother-bird had cruelly thrown the little strangers from the nest. Our all-wise cook was of the opinion that I should kill the four survivors. " Birds," he said, " are vermin. . . . It is also a bad omen to have birds nesting under your roof."

The bullock-cart had just returned from Nymba. The cook who was always very curious to see what had been brought from the shops, stood at the foot of the verandah ready to open the parcels for me. There were two from England. (I always insisted upon parcels being opened out of doors, for they invariably harboured a swarm of cockroaches which were immediately killed by the cook, who squashed them lustily beneath his horny heels !) Books and magazines brought back the blessings of a life which we had not properly appreciated. " What's in that parcel ? " the cook would politely ask when mail-day arrived. He did so want to know. Sometimes there were toys, mechanical frogs and musical instruments, or perhaps a couple of desirable shirts. Whatever it was, it was worth seeing, and it became a sort of ritual to unpack these European packages under supervision of the cook, the houseboy and the Masai ' herd.' They seemed to test the spirit of my generosity by staring mutely at my gifts from home. I knew that in the case of a toy taking their fancy, it would in a few days' time disappear from Marie's collection, never to be seen again. . . .

There was a letter from a stranger, too, who knew a friend of a friend whom we had not seen for many years and who wanted us to tell them whether we considered it wise to rctirc to Kenya on an income of £300 per annum. It was said that one could live cheaper in Kenya than at home. . . . " Another mug," said John, as he gave me back the letter. It was difficult to conceive anyone wishing to leave their country—without, that is, having to do so !

I visualized the life that this elderly couple could lead in health and peace in a cottage at home ; the garden they could cultivate, the social life which even on a small income could be theirs, the comforts of a modern home they could enjoy with good food, books, music and the glorious change of seasons.

It was, of course, possible to live without any money at all in Kenya. The gentleman who had temporarily camped in our house before our arrival, did in fact do so. He had not a penny and lived entirely by his wits, which was not very difficult in a country where White people are hospitable and the natives simple. Occasionally he sent his servant to borrow our shot-gun but had never yet called upon us himself. He had built a grass hut on the brow of the escarpment, and lived from hand to mouth. It was said that he had been an officer in the Guards. Since those far-off days he had done many things. Amongst his many qualifications he had become a Mohammedan, which endeared him to the Indian shopkeepers who gave him unlimited credit. He had, so the rumour went, been deported several times but by some artifice invariably returned again, swimming ashore at some port or other, walking through the Sudan—anything to return to the country where he knew he could manage to live without money. He had even been to prison, thus causing the local authorities much trouble, for he was the only White man in detention. The prestige of the White man having of necessity to be upheld, he was given a job as overseer—a position he much enjoyed. So much so that he frequently tried to be sent back to gaol again, to the comparative comforts of what he called " Government service." A White man could go native and live on potatoes and bananas, providing that he could manage to keep well ; providing, too, that his finer nature was comfortably dead. . . .

In due course I had an opportunity of knowing this ex-officer of the Guards. It came about in this way. John was obliged to go to Nymba for a couple of days, and after my experience with the drunken manager and the black mamba (experiences which recurred again and again in my dreams) I very much disliked being left alone, even for a single night. John therefore went to call on Mr. Smith-Smythe in his hut, several miles to the north, and asked him would he mind looking after me and the child during his absence. John was loath to ask for this help and had argued with me before he went and had given me some lessons in how to use an automatic revolver. But it was no use ; I hated handling any kind of gun ; besides, I could never hit even the biggest target. Mr. Smith-Smythe, John said, accepted willingly.

I ordered a nice dinner and opened the last remaining tins of peas, tomato-soup and fruit which we had kept since Christmas. They were gifts from home and carefully kept for emergencies.  There was a full bottle of whisky on the sideboard and I had for the first time unpacked my coffee percolator, much to the joy of the houseboy, who fairly revelled in anything bright and shiny.  Mr. S.-S. duly arrived with his servant following behind, carrying his suit-case—a dilapidated affair, covered with pre-war labels.  My guest was an impressive man ; tall, well-built and with a shock of curly white hair. There was an air of great dignity about him.  His manner was perfect . . . it was more than that, it belonged to an age that had gone.  He bowed, he begged my pardon, he darted at the door-handle at every opportunity.  At sunset he retired to his room, had a bath and changed into an ancient dinner-jacket which reached half-way to his knees.  His slightly yellow shirt had once been good.  He was shaved and his hair was beautifully brushed.  He really looked magnificent.  He bowed charmingly and said : " After you, Madam . . ." or " Upon my word, dear lady."  Indeed, the man and his conversation seemed unreal.  It was as though he had stepped out of the past.

Modestly he referred to his explorations in the jungle of Brazil, the alligators he had escaped from, the Indians who had been on the verge of murdering him. . . . He was a splendid failure and an amazing actor ; he was never dull and never seemed to brag. . . . He referred to his former position in the Government.  I felt as if I were taking part in a play.  Talking charmingly of this and that, his eyes devoured the food and then slowly wandered to the sideboard. . . . He grew still more chatty : " When I struck up the Amazon," he began, or " When I lay in hiding from the natives, for weeks, dying of hunger and thirst, my most loyal servant," and so on.

After dinner he picked up my wrap and delicately laid it over my shoulders. We had coffee on the verandah. The moon had disappeared and left us in partial darkness. Natives flitted by noiselessly, barefoot, to some nightly sing-song. They seemed like spirits. . . . In the darkness he told me of still further impossible adventures. He would have made a brilliant lecturer, the kind that sometimes talks to young men in Y.M.C.A.s or to older men in suburban Bible-classes. He had, I realised with wonder, found life completely satisfying. Never once had he been disenchanted. He talked with profound conviction. One was compelled to listen ; his technique was perfect. Born *raconteur* that he was, I wondered how he could happily endure such solitude, for his only audience were natives. Mr. S.-S. spoke Swahili perfectly and probably entertained them with his talk, for they all adored him. He was also the only man I ever met who contrived to be perfectly content doing absolutely nothing at all. Never did he find life futile or despairing, even though he did not own a single thing. To him death did not loom ahead as the only possible change from any empty existence. He had had a colourful life, a wife or two somewhere in the distant past, and now he was well over sixty, which is, I reckon, the age of contentment. . . . He was never really short of food. The natives kept him in tobacco ; the Mohammedan shopkeepers in drink. White men were less generous. He became a blood-brother here and a blood-brother there. It was as good as a life-insurance. I said good-night at ten o'clock. Courteously he accompanied me to my bedroom door, opened it for me and then returned once more to the verandah where he smoked and drank whisky. Politely and without vulgar haste he sipped it until every drop had gone ; my second and last bottle of precious whisky ! We never bought another for we could not afford it. The cook brought the empty bottle to my room with my morning cup of tea. " *Kuisha*," he said, " *kafiza*." (Finished—completely.)

# XXIII

U P AT 7 A.M. AND SPARKLING WITH HEALTH and vigour, the remarkable Mr. S.-S. had been down by the lake to have a shot at wild duck with John's shotgun. He returned bright and hatless, glad to be alive. A new day to him, even in that seventh hell, was anything but a vacuum. The whisky had had no ill effects. The tropics never downed him, nor did the poisonous home-grown tobacco. His life seemed to be charmed. He was, indeed, the only perfectly healthy White man I ever met in Kenya. Slung over his unpaid servant's back was a pelican, an enormous bird, weighing about three stone. At first the cook flatly refused to pluck it, but remembering his docile wife, he took it to her hut. It proved tough eating though. My guest declined to stop for lunch, seeing that there was no more whisky. He had, I fear, no shame. With elaborate thanks he departed to " his place," borrowing John's gun just for a day or two and filling his pockets with cartridges.

" Any time, dear lady," he said, " that I can be of any use to you, do just send word."

We did get the gun back eventually, but only after many futile attempts to find him in his hut. It appeared that he had again returned to " Government service " shortly afterwards. . . .

John arrived home at tea-time with the most exciting news. He had bought a couple of mules and a buggy !

The manager of Nymba's Grand Hotel had sold them to him cheap. There were other things, of course, than mules which were at the moment more urgently needed. There was the overdraft not yet wiped out and there was, too, the everlasting need for further oxen. . . . There was also that other plough, that second team we should have had, but in the meanwhile we had to live and what was more, we needed to get about in order to keep in touch with other human beings. Things were looking up, I thought. There was some further news, equally exciting. Another White man was on his way who had bought a thousand acres of land only a mile or so from us. John had met him in the hotel lounge. " Very decent young chap," was his opinion.

John had in his desperate fit of extravagance also bought some wood for a sitting-room floor. My happiness was almost complete ! My conscience was untroubled by the apparent extravagance ; besides, we argued, we could always sell the mules again if necessary. Ill-provided as we were with creature comforts, we had grown to look upon almost anything as a luxury. By the storehouse stood our lofty buggy with its narrow springless seat. Two shaggy mules were grazing happily on the plain, looking already thoroughly at home.

" They are tired now," said John, " but, by jove, they're not as phlegmatic as they look. Twice they bolted across the stream as I came along. . . ."

Recalling an invitation a lady had given me in the hotel lounge when Marie had ophthalmia, we decided to pay her a call on the following Saturday afternoon. After all, it was not far to go now that we had the mules. Twenty-five miles to a neighbouring valley could be done in about four hours. We started early, after a great deal of trouble with the mules, which had

to be held down by several natives, as they were rear-
ing and kicking long before they were hitched to the
buggy. Bolting down the road, dodging trees, or
driving through rough ground soon tired them
though. Going across country, bumping into hog
and ant-bear holes, disturbing wild pigs and crashing
through a nest of ostrich eggs was very exciting—at
first. One of the mules, by name " Ginger," was for
ever wanting to return home ; his bump of locality
was amazing. . . . Skirting one of the hills, we were
booed by a family of baboons which was evidently
doing some rock-climbing and evidently did not like
the look of us ! There was a river running through
this valley which in the dry season was almost non-
existent, but during the rains it became a raging
torrent. This valley had a bad name, even as far
down as Nairobi. It was maize country mostly, and
fever-stricken, one of the hostile valleys which rejected
the tiller of the soil and slowly broke his heart. Even
the settlers living there were known to be " queer " ;
given to strange habits, violent outbursts and
unsociability.

We came upon an unusually lengthy well-made
drive leading up to my friend's house. There were
rows of eucalyptus trees on either side as well as
several rambling rose-trees. The place looked utterly
deserted. The silence was slightly uncanny ; there
was no cracking of a whip, no ploughing being done
and not a single farm-hand anywhere. Ginger
shied at nothing once or twice, and Brownie, his
companion, was also showing signs of nerves. . . .
An old Kikuyu who was driving a goat along the path,
crossed to the other side without apparent interest
in us.

" Where is your master ? " John called out to him.
Reluctantly the negro came across.

" The Master ? " he asked, " didn't you know that he has gone ? *quenda, quenda kafiza,* gone away for good ? "

" Gone where ? "

" *Sijui,* don't know ; *Uleia,* White man's country I expect," he said vaguely pointing to the far horizon.

" Where is the *Memsahib?* " I wanted to know, hoping that at least she would be in.

" *Memsahib ?* " he shook his head, " *Memsahib na kufa,* she is dead."

It was evident that everything had been left in a hurry ; deserted just as it stood. A couple of ploughs stood crookedly in the middle of a field, a wagon had been left on the plough land—abandoned—yet looking for all the world as if they expected to be called back to life at any moment. In a flash the lives of my friend and her husband seemed to have been bared of all. . . . It was not long since I had listened to her playing the piano in the hotel lounge. She had been playing Chopin's Preludes on the old piano which was not merely out of tune, but which did not sound the centre octave. We had been trying some duets together, thoroughly enjoying ourselves, as neither of us had a piano on our farms. She had been telling me of their coming holiday at home in England after a seven years' effort to save a hundred and fifty pounds.

" There is her grave," said the Kikuyu, pointing to a mound of earth which was covered with a pile of stones, which looked white in the glare of the sun . . . a dreary thorn bush shading it indifferently. Could anyone, I asked myself, know peace in such a place ?

" The master buried her himself. Smallpox," the old man added, and then he spat and walked away.

This was the most haunting tragedy I had ever

come across—and still the African sun smiled its
everlasting ugly grin. This wilderness, so alien—
how I began to hate it ! Death, I felt, was infinitely
more brutal if met in such a place. The very grave
in this desolation seemed to mock the thought of
peace. It looked unspeakably solemn and forlorn.
There was not a single flower within miles that I
might pluck to place on it. . . . The book that Mrs.
X had been reading still lay open on a chair. A cup
and saucer stood on the table ; the door of the wardrobe was open and clothes lay scattered over the
chintz-covered chairs. The house was not even
locked. Weeds were spreading in profusion everywhere and the verandah was covered with dust.

" Come away," John called crossly as he turned the
buggy.

" Homeward " we trotted. For three solid hours
no word passed between us. But we were thinking.
. . . The sun shone at the slant as we passed the
Simba lake, revealing a certain amount of colouring.
But it was a short-lived transformation, for the sun
slipped behind the horizon almost at once. The
great-grandmother of the head-*shamba* boy's latest
baby squatted on her haunches outside her hut as
we passed, suckling her great-grandchild. She was
still with milk, it seemed. After all, I reckoned that
she was probably only forty-two years old. . . .

## XXIV

OUR NEW NEIGHBOUR ARRIVED WITH A GREAT DEAL
of to-do. He too had brought a bullock-wagon, very
much second-hand, laden high with his belongings.
Eight undersized oxen led the way. There was a
plough, a mountain of metal like a scrap-heap piled
up in the rear of the wagon, and a meagre cow
trailing behind. The young man had a big-brimmed
felt-hat pushed well to the back of his head, whilst
over his shoulder he had a rifle, an enormous rifle
it looked. The axles of his wagon seemed to be in
dire need of oil. The screech of the revolving wheels
sounded infinitely monotonous as the wagon passed
along at great leisure.

The procession went clattering down the incline
to the stream, thus suddenly changing its tune. Too
sleepy to drink I expect, the oxen lugged the cart up
again to the other side and again the *rat-tat-tat* and
shriek were repeated, until eventually it faded away
into the distance. Looking down from the altitude
of our own dearly-bought experience and watching
that lonely White man disappear into the distance
behind his ludicrous outfit, I felt profoundly sorry for
him. His venture, like ours, seemed slightly comical
—and like ours, doomed to failure? I took out my
field-glasses and watched the outfit wander on into
the gleaming distance followed by a worried-looking
cow, swinging pathetically-inadequate udders, and
a very young man, straight from home, preoccupied

149

with his thoughts, looking neither to the right nor left.

Bravely he stepped into this new world of his, not yet aware of its desolation. I nearly hailed him, but thought better of it. . . . The outfit stopped by the swamp and I could see the young man sitting down on the wagon contemplating his new environment. Perhaps (who knows?) he thought it lovely, full of wonderful bird-life, romantic, a drinking-place for wild creatures, for there beneath him in the mud were the tracks of buffaloes, water-buck and many other dwellers of the wild.

We called on him a fortnight later. Walking carefully for fear of snakes through the waving dry grass, we descended further into the burning furnace of the Simba valley. How that hot wind blew! We passed our oxen grazing by the stream. They had grown somewhat gaunt of late, owing to the lack of fresh green grass. Bill's (for that was what we called him when we knew him well enough) place, which he had just finished building, was almost like a dugout. He had built a one-roomed house of wire netting, over which he plastered mud which was conditioned with cowdung, because of its binding properties. Now it was getting dry and already there were cracks through which one could see the sunshine. In the darkest corner of this room stood his shabby bed and home-made bookshelf. On it lay his Bible, a gift from his mother, some dusty papers on agriculture and a faded photograph of his home, a beautiful ivy-covered country-house in Surrey. Adjoining his room was a corrugated-iron lean-to where a couple of chipped enamel cooking pans reposed on an up-turned box. On the floor stood a primus stove down which it was evident that innumerable meals had boiled over. Bill, a stocky young fellow, was sitting by the home-made table eating his lunch, or dinner, whichever it was, at four o'clock in the afternoon. Banana pudding. He had his hat on, as the roof did not keep out the sun. He was very pleased to see us. " This is my fourth banana pudding this week," he announced, laughing.

Bananas everywhere, and not a thing to eat ! Still, Bill's heart was brave like John's, and somehow or another he was going to make good. It would cost so little, he thought, to keep himself. It appeared that he had even less money than we, but his farm was the same size as ours and had been purchased from the same owner. So far he seemed to have done nothing except lay out a very tidy little vegetable garden in the shade of some trees. There was a hard-baked wall of clay at the back of his house, which led up sheer to the escarpment above. He kept a pack of dogs, lean and hungry brutes they looked, which he needed he said, for company. There was no one else to talk to. . . .

Bill was only twenty-one ! At this tender age he should have had a little more out of life than his own company. An unexpected visit could bring forth nothing from his store, for he had nothing to offer. Bread there was, like indiarubber ; butter made in a bottle, and sometimes plum jam, so he said. He only had two cups and one spoon, one chair and one packing-case. He appeared too lackadaisical to improve his comforts. He was interested, though, in vegetables. He had, he went on to tell us, taken a course of market-gardening in England. Suffering greatly from indigestion he was going to live on vegetables. The herd boy would cook for him in his spare time.

" There's no art," he declared " in cooking green stuff."

" But what about bread ? " I asked.

" Bread ? " he replied, for the first time appearing to notice his loaf which looked grey and solid, " it hasn't risen, has it ? "

Bill told us of his plans ; how many acres of coffee he would grow and how many acres of maize. He would also build a stone house, would get an Indian stonemason down to do it.

He did indeed start to build a house after a year or two and he did have an Indian stonemason down— but he never finished it. It did not appear worth-while, even though the rains had washed away the mud from the wire-netting of his hut until it looked exactly like a chicken run, leaving free access to mosquitoes and other nameless insects to enter. Twice his roof had blown away and for several days he did not even bother to replace it. Nearly all his oxen had died of East-Coast fever and for a long time he had no beasts at all. . . . There were barren months and years ahead which he experienced in greater solitude than we, blank periods marked by nothing except the joyous expectancy of mail-days. But Bill was not the complaining kind. Unaware of his hard life, his people were equally ignorant of the fact that an extra hundred pounds or two might have almost changed his destiny. . . . Snapshots arrived from home of friends playing tennis in his mother's garden. Little would they have believed that even in Kenya itself there were many people who had no idea how people like us and Bill lived ! Many of them, of course, had more money than us to spend on luxuries : books safari-going, food, gramophones and motor-cars. Most, too, were sure of going home on leave once in three years. . . .

It made me smile when I looked back, when I remembered the things I had imagined about Kenya

before we had left our house in the Avenue in Mannington. I pictured myself walking out in the dewy
morning for a dip in the stream, breathing the aroma-
tic air of cedar woods, enjoying the company of
charming, congenial neighbours ; of a health-giving
life, a life of beauty and freedom. The grim reality
was that I went short walks through featureless
scenery, taking my baby with me, for I could never
leave her safely at home. It was anything but
romantic. . . .

There were now Bill's seventy-five books to read,
which took me exactly three months, including those
on gardening, lowbrow love-stories, detective-yarns
and a medical book with lurid illustrations of every
possible human ailment and so vividly described that
I suffered in turn from hookworm, insanity and per-
nicious anæmia ! I also read the whole of the Bible
at frequent intervals. There was, indeed, very little
else to occupy my time. The days and weeks and
months seemed like eternity. The Kenya of my
dreams, the country of my fertile imagination,
crashed to pieces. We weren't making any money.
We were not going to make any money either, nor
was Bill. The park-like beauty of Kenya existed only
in the highlands, ten to twelve thousand feet above
the sea. Our land in the valley did not yield the fruits
of our labour, nor indeed were there any care-free
gatherings of neighbours in the cool of the evening
that one had fondly imagined. In short, life was far
from idyllic. . . .

Still, there was Marie, who had now become the
biggest joy in our lonely existence—an existence
which was not kind to the child. She not only showed
signs of anæmia but had had dysentery and sunstroke,
ophthalmia and other, minor, ailments. Sometimes I
grew frightened for with something akin to panic

I realised that for short spells I completely lost my memory. I felt that I could not tell John, for fear of worrying him unduly. Perhaps he, too, experienced the same lapses. I could not, for instance, be sure whether it was morning or afternoon ; whether we had eaten lunch, or what exactly I had been doing since I had got up. Oftentimes I had no idea what month of the year it was or, for that matter, what year it was. From all accounts this was not an unusual mental state to be in, even for the very young.

John, who may have realised that this was no sort of life for a woman, surprised me one day with a crate of sixty fowls. They were to be my very own.

" It will give you no end of an interest," he said encouragingly.

The birds were small and bedraggled, the native variety, and said to be tough and always hungry. Still, I was very pleased to have them, in spite of my secret conviction that live things in Kenya invariably became a liability. The fowls at least kept us well provided with eggs and the quality of our food accordingly rose by leaps and bounds. We did not economise with the eggs and there was no end to the experiments our cook made ! John erected a beautiful fence round the poultry-yard, burying the netting in the ground in order to prevent unwelcome strangers from crawling in. Marie and I, carrying basins full of maize, fed them happily twice a day. But the birds did not respond to our approach with enthusiasm ; they seemed to take it all as a matter of course, even as they regarded the little stream which we carefully led through the poultry-run. The whole concern, I discovered before a month was out, was but another of these numerous outrageous losses suffered by the enterprising farmer in Kenya. It was a common experience that hawks, suspended in the air, would suddenly swoop down and wantonly snatch up a hen. They seemed to have become aware of the easy access to our poultry-yard and they swooped down and vanished again with a chicken snatched from the very circle of its family. That was in the daytime. At night a mongoose actually dug a trench underneath the fencing and killed thirty-six chickens during one single visit. Thirty-six dead chicks wounded in the neck where the mongoose had sucked their blood, lay in the sun. We did not know what to do with them. But the natives gladly solved the problem and came begging to be given a welcome change in their monotonous diet.

I'm afraid that I was now beginning to lose my temper at the slightest provocation and had continually to hold myself in check.

" John," I said, viewing the thirty-six corpses with tears in my eyes, " if you had had any sense you would have bought me a dozen new gramophone records instead."

Hardly caring what happened to the rest of the poultry, I unaccountably found them to thrive for a spell. Three of them, however, were eaten by a snake which afterwards sunned itself on a rock, disgustingly distended. But the cook, who liked nothing better than to kill snakes, ended its life before it had digested its meal !

Still the little brook gurgled past the hencoop and the cock crowed merrily, though there seemed but little to crow about now. Exactly two months later—almost to my relief—I lost them all. They succumbed, without the slightest battle, to a mysterious chicken disease. I doctored them with Epsom salts, which I fear only hastened their end. Our puddings were less-nourishing after that, nor were there any more cakes. I again bought my eggs from the natives, who seemed invariably luckier with fowls than White people. Perhaps it was because they shared their huts with them. The last remaining cockerel which survived the chicken-diarrhœa now had the whole run to himself. He must have felt with a vengeance that he owned the " open spaces " ! But his end, too, was imminent. He was mercifully snatched away by a hawk. . . . I watched him disappear away in the hazy sky behind the Aberdares. Thus, dramatically, ended my short-lived chicken-venture.

## XXV

Our fourth Christmas had come round and gone. We were again heavily in debt. Still, the rains would soon be due and now we had forty-odd acres of land ready for sowing. Yet, we were getting wiser, and lurking at the back of our minds was the conviction that we were wasting our lives.

The batch of mail which arrived from home each month conveyed to us in some subtle way the need of justifying our enterprise. It was *expected* of us. As though we were not trying! Lying awake at night an unpleasant critical-faculty, which I had gradually developed, could no longer be subdued. Perhaps, I thought, that mile-long saltlick by the lake was some day yet going to make our fortune. Our oxen thrived, thin though they were, and we put it down to the salt. Two farmers from the upper valley had twice sent some of their cattle down to us to recuperate. This brought in just a little money. But the " treatment " seemed to pick them up no end. They were nibbling the charred tufts of grass, followed by a flock of egrets which perched on their backs, picking ticks from their patchy coats. Bill and John had so far, as a whole, lost far less cattle than the farmers did on their higher altitudes. . . .

Bill was getting quarrelsome, and John was also quick to fly into a temper. It was not, of course, to be surprised at. Everybody we heard of, up the valley and elsewhere, had at some time or other had a row with their neighbours whilst many were not on speaking terms. Until one had lived in these parts one fondly imagined that such misdemeanours as cheating or trying to get the better of one's neighbour was not done in these outposts of the Empire where there was, according to one's preconceived ideas, a sort of bond between exiled brothers ! It was, alas, the very opposite. Neighbours had a habit of sending offensive notes about trifling matters and imaginary happenings, accusing some innocent, for instance, of allowing his men or cattle or mules to wander on to their farms. One fellow actually shot his own mule which he found wandering amongst his corn, thinking that it belonged to his neighbour ! They boxed their own and their neighbours' servants' ears if they failed to be servile enough, which in their childlike simplicity they sometimes forgot to be. Some were proud, I know, as proud as the White man—and some had even more reason to be.

White men coolly cut off one's water-supply, if they happened to live nearer to the source of the stream and wanted to irrigate their dying crops. One could, of course, go to law about it but there were those preliminary notes oozing misery and hatred, whilst in any case the damage had been done to one's own crops. The unwritten law of helpfulness in exiled places that one read about in pre-war novels, existed only in story-books! People living in towns were almost always far more thoughtful of their neighbours.

Sometimes I felt so weak that I had barely the strength to walk from room to room ; it was partly through lack of exercise, as well as low-fever. I made myself walk, yet there seemed nowhere to go with a child. There was no road, barely a footpath even leading into the bush where it was not always safe to go with a youngster. We had already met a lioness, numerous snakes as well as wart-hogs. Twice we had met a family of baboons. . . . Daily we walked to the vegetable-garden gathering cape-gooseberries, wearily removing a handful of weeds, examining the one and only orange we managed to grow, which was subsequently stolen before it was ripe. I felt like a drone, bone-idle and useless. I also tried to grow a rose-tree, and it looked as if it might have great possibilities. I had sent for it to Nairobi, in one of those desperate fits of extravagance that poor people in Kenya so often display. It did produce one single bloom, which lasted but for a day. I trained it to grow up on one of the wooden pillars of the verandah. Why I encouraged more foliage to cover the house with I cannot imagine, for as it was the spreading branches of the eucalyptus trees harboured quantities of green snakes which every now and then dropped on to the floor frightening me to death. I would be sitting sewing, when from beneath my camp-chair, just by my feet, a snake would slowly make its way, nosing in and out of my sewing-basket. There was nothing to be done except sit still until the danger had passed. . . .

One of our young cows had calved during the night, with the help of our faithful Masai. But it was another loss, for the cow had to be killed as she was unable to feed her calf because of a diseased udder. Her *moo-ing* was pitiful to hear until we could stand it no longer. John shot her at sunset, just as the day's work was done. Like the doctor, the veterinary-surgeon lived too far away to be of any real use to us.

It was at sundown that the men returned from their labours, each with a spade over his shoulder. They sang as they came. They always did. Indeed, it was the most cheerful thing in the whole of Africa, that happy, hopeful singing of the natives. The oxen were driven into their *bomas* while the natives crept into their smoke-filled huts. They always lit their fires indoors, and as there was no outlet for the smoke, it gradually filtered through the thatch. Sometimes I met Bill on his rounds, whilst occasionally he came round to beg me to cut his hair for him, which was curling down his neck and over his ears like a woman's.

"What a happy-go-lucky existence!" he exclaimed, as I snipped a piece of flesh from the top of his ear.

"Happy-go-lucky, forsooth!" I replied banteringly.

Bill looked at me as though he wanted me to contradict him; he seemed to be ready for an argument, for he still defended his present mode of life with all the ferocity of an anxious man. He had grown very thin and pasty-looking, and his back was slightly bent.

"I'd be sick and tired living in a city," he went on. "Fancy being cooped up in an office! Why, look at this stretch of country now, and then just look at it again in two or three years' time. You'll not be able to recognise it. You'll see acres and acres of maize and rows and rows of coffee-trees. I'll build a house, as well; a good one, and then I'll lay a tennis court. What young man, I ask you, has such opportunities at home?"

I was beginning to ask myself whether Bill were not suffering from sunstroke—his youthful boasting seemed abnormal. After I had cut his hair we walked through a patch of forest along a very narrow track, which had been worn through the undergrowth by generations of big game. We came out on to the plain which lay dazzling in the sun. In the distance I could see John working in the ploughed field. Natives were weeding, weeding all the time, between the scanty rows of slow-growing coffee-bushes. The weeds were as tough as wire-netting, choking everything which came within their reach. Barely had the men come to the end of a row than weeds sprouted up again at the other end !

" My old man," said Bill, " was very keen for me to come out here. You see, he spent part of his life in Australia ; a long time ago though, about fifty years ago. He did well and he says that he'd give anything to have his time all over again."

" They always do, at his age," I put in bitterly. " Besides, I have no objection to old people emigrating, especially those who have had their fun. Let them all emigrate and make room for the young ones at home, whose enthusiasm, *joie-de-vivre*, still run high. They might make a success of the Old Country yet."

It was now Bill's turn to think that I was suffering from sunstroke. . . .

The rains were somewhat overdue and Bill's vegetable-patch looked very sick. Numerous fires had burnt the grass for miles around and the landscape looked black. Ashes blew sky-high and covered the trees. But Bill did not seem to notice. Perhaps it was because he was a man. He was here and he was determined to like it at all costs. It seemed to make him cross, though ! His two decent suits which had long ago been eaten by rats and white ants, cut him off from civilisation. There was, I thought, a great deal of make-belief in peoples' lives, and it took more courage than was generally realised to face up to and admit the truth. When I studied those who called Kenya beautiful, the opinion seemed mostly to come from the wealthy, the sport-loving and those who had no other choice. Their illnesses, their insane tempers, their anæmic children—everything belied their statements. The health and what seemed to me the mental condition of my acquaintances (as well as myself), gave me a great deal to think about.

A White man, who had lately taken over the farm where the two former owners had both committed suicide, had, so the passing policeman declared, tied a negro to a tree and flogged him until the poor wretch fell unconscious. Why the negro failed to complain I do not know, for flogging was, of course, against the law. Few natives, however, stood up for their rights; perhaps they were too shy. I saw the boy later, whose body still showed signs of the festering weals of the whip. He had come to beg for some boracic powder, which I freely applied to his wounds. The same man had also flogged a boy of ours for some trifling, barely-understood offence. Privation, solitude, lack of varied food, badly-cooked food, sun and fever—all left their mark on a man.

Bill was now only twenty-one, and in urgent need of assistance, mostly financially, of course. But like most young men, he never told his people. (There is no sacrifice so selfless, so utterly sanguine as that of the young.) His dogs ran wild, at times they were ravenous, and howled all through the night. Several times they attempted to eat our home-cured leather harness—and almost succeeded. Lean hounds they were, tick-ridden and wild-eyed. Bill would have been better off had he been married and could have shared his burden . . . but these were idle speculations, considering that most wives in our and neighbouring valleys were constantly leaving their men to fend for themselves, while they themselves went off to Europe or had a good time in Nairobi—or worse still, perhaps, left for good. Women in Kenya were still scarce and much sought after.

The rains started with a thunderbolt. It was the

first rains Bill experienced and he, too, immediately started to sow with newborn energy. His oxen, three of them, got " blown." They lay on the ground with their bellies enormously distended. I came upon him giving one of them an enema, one of these small rubber-ball affairs which his mother had packed at the bottom of his trunk for his own private use ! It must have acted on the ox like a drop in the ocean ! Priding myself upon my superior experience, I showed him whereabouts in the beast's side our oxen had been successfully stabbed and thus relieved of gas. Bill took out his pocket-knife and gravely contemplated its numerous gadgets. There was a corkscrew, a tin-opener, but the blades were rather short. With the courage and the gambling-spirit of a surgeon, Bill decided to risk it. After all, there was no other cure. I turned my back and then suddenly heard a sound resembling an enormous sigh. Like the air from a motor-tyre, the gas escaped from the animal, which immediately rose to its feet again and promptly began to eat. The three operations were entirely successful, and Bill felt like patting himself on the back.

# XXVI

THE MAIZE THIS YEAR LOOKED HEALTHY AND WAS a ovely green. Anxiously we watched the sky, forever fearing another drought. Early one afternoon at the end of the second month the sun grew strangely obscured. A deep gloom covered the earth. The sky was obscured with a red cloud, which, with a curious humming sound, rapidly descended upon us.

The locusts had come.

Nothing could stop them now. How could mere man control this cloud of destruction? There was no effective way of attacking it. As the voracious insects started on their work of absolute desolation, John ordered the men to light a bonfire, hoping thereby to smoke them out. But it had not the slightest effect. The cook, frantically hammering saucepan lids together, tried to frighten off this dreadful visitation. The maize as well as our vegetables were being devoured under our very eyes. . . . John did not seem unduly upset. He was getting surprisingly imperturbable. " It just couldn't be helped," was all he said, as he toyed with his dinner.

The natives fairly gorged on locusts; to such an extent, in fact, that they required dosing with castor-oil. Once more our trust in Kenya was betrayed, but we bore the blow most philosophically. Making a living in Kenya was altogether too grim an affair to be taken too tragically. Perhaps, after all, Mr.

Smith-Smythe was the only White man who knew the secret of happiness. . . .

Once more living up to the hilt of our overdraft, I decided to do the usual thing—to take in lodgers, for I had seen the following advertisement in a weekly paper : " Lady with two small children would like to live on farm as paying guest, three months."

Leaving John behind to build a mill to be driven by the waterfall, I took the mules and buggy and drove to Nymba to meet the lady and to discuss the matter and to bring her down the valley if we came to an agreement. It was a thrilling ride. Behind me on my suitcase sat a native whose duty it was to look after the mules. We were jolted from right to left, occasionally being almost thrown out of our seats. The grassland looked level enough to the eye, but on wheels it was another matter ! We had to cross three different river-beds and the water was high, reaching the driver's seat. Twice the mules shied : once for no reason at all, and the second time at the approach of a motor-car on the main road to Nymba. We fairly skimmed past trees and bullock-wagons and dawdling natives. Time, the eternal bugbear of White people, did not seem to exist for them. They had not the faintest desire as a rule to get to a place quickly, whilst they simply did not understand being punished for loitering on the way.

My first goal after arriving at the hotel-yard was usually to the post-office. It was as though I expected something from home, some news which would miraculously bring us release. It was exciting enough, though, to receive odd packages of papers. Invariably I expected the most amazing changes to have taken place, and it was almost depressing to observe that life had gone on in the same dull way. Busy with its own difficulties, England seemed to have forgotten us. . . . The only things which noticeably changed (according to the papers) were the ladies' fashions and which made me feel distinctly dowdy. There was a letter, too, for John, which made me smile. His father had sent him eight pounds to go away with for a holiday ! One might have gone to Brighton for a few days on that, or to an apartment house in Blackpool, but in Kenya it simply took you nowhere !

Musing on holidays, reminded me again of the extreme unsoundness of our financial position. The question arose : should I with this windfall of eight pounds in my hands buy John a couple of shirts, the old ones being in holes, or should I again accept the hospitality of the local club without becoming a member, or should I go to the hospital to have one of my most useful molars drawn, which had given me much pain lately ? It had suddenly become tremendously important that the lady with her two children should consent to come—which in view of the fact that I had only one bedroom to offer and that I should be obliged to mention the abundance of mosquitoes—was doubtful. The room did not even possess a wardrobe, and the other furniture was partially home-made. Sitting in the hotel lounge, which had been painted in a dull brown, I listened to a young man playing the tinny piano. The tunes he played were exactly five years old. Two other fellows lounged heavily on the springless sofa. One of them, a middle-aged man, was evidently just off down the Simba valley.

" Old Marriott wants me to survey that land north of the Simba swamp," he announced. " I wouldn't live down there for anything. As a matter of fact, I have a strong suspicion that it is on the very fringe of the dry belt which appears to stretch from the Simba swamp, past Lake Rudolf to the border of Abyssinia. I believe that a so-called dry belt is not a stationary thing, but is apt to encroach in the same way as the sea encroaches on the land."

" Are you sure," said the young man, turning round on the piano-stool, " that it's encroaching only there ? To me it seems damned uncertain everywhere. As long as I've been here we haven't had the rain we needed."

Another elderly man opened the door. He stood on the doorstep a moment or two but did not speak. His clothes were shabby. From the torn elbows of his ancient cardigan two very bony arms protruded. His face was remarkable for its look of intelligence. Two piercingly dark eyes darted here and there, and then he turned and walked to the other door where it said " Bar."

" Do you know the old boy ? " asked the Surveyor.

" No, who is he ? "

" That's the famous Lord X."

" Jove ! " said the fellow by the piano, " why doesn't someone patch his clothes ? "

" He's been here since 1890," said the first.

" Must have liked the place."

" Don't know about that ; he just wouldn't be licked. He's said to have lost hundreds of thousands of pounds at one time or another—tried everything. Whatever he went in for, something cropped up sooner or later and ruined it for him. Clever chap though. It's a mighty thin line, I always think, which divides failure from success. He kept on coming back again and again just to have another shot at it. He's still experimenting, as far as I know. He'll make his fortune yet—out of land, though."

Next morning I called at the hospital to have my

tooth drawn. The doctor was away on a fortnight's holiday. The Indian doctor had also left, for good. The place seemed to have been left in charge of some black male nurses. The sun fairly poured down on the hospital roof, the pepper-trees drooped, so did the languid patients who squatted outside their huts. On my way back I met the bank manager's harassed little wife who asked me in to lunch. Out of her bemirrored sideboard she took a bottle of port and poured me out a glass. " It will deaden the tooth-ache," she persuaded. It did. Since I was completely unused to alcohol in any form, the wine had the most unexpected effect upon me. For an hour and a half I was unable to leave the chair! The room swayed gently; someone spoke to me from a great distance apparently. Presently my good little Samaritan, feeling rather worried, sent for her husband, who promptly went across to the hotel to fetch an Indian Army doctor who was on his way touring the country. I often wondered if he ever guessed my true condition. He took me back to the hospital in his car and asked to be given the forceps, a needle and some cocaine. He pushed me gently into a chair, turned up his shirt sleeves and asked me to show him the offending tooth. The male nurse returned with the instruments on a tray.

" Sorry, sir," he said, " we have no needle, it's broken."

This seemed to me by no means an unusual predica-ment of Nymba's General Hospital.

" Never mind," replied the doctor, " you hold the lady's head." To me : " I'm afraid I shall have to hurt you," he smiled while he struggled with the tooth, pulling it from right to left in a desperate attempt to get it out. He hated doing it ; he wasn't in the habit of doing it either, by all appearances.

John I felt could have done it better. Perspiring profusely he eventually produced a tooth and I vaguely hoped that it was the right one. Several other teeth on either side of the extracted tooth had been thoroughly loosened as well. Taking me back to the hotel he told me to lie down. He also invited me to dinner that night, which I gladly accepted, having been starved of company for so long.

" I'm terribly sorry," he repeated several times during dinner, referring to his job in the morning. He seemed to think I was a great object for pity. I noticed, however, that he offered me no wine. Gradually I began to tell him of our experiences ; of our four years' struggle. . . . It did me an enormous lot of good to get it off my chest for once.

" Well, since you ask me what I should do in your position, I should say that the most intelligent—in fact, the only rational—thing to do would be to sell out to some other young fools and go elsewhere."

Blunt though the advice was, I knew it was sound. John, however, would hesitate to admit that he was licked ; he would go on hoping and hoping till doomsday, and probably lose his money altogether.

The lady with the two children arrived from Nairobi by the midnight train. Her two little boys, twins, could be heard screaming all over the hotel. Some one called out " Shut up ! ", a door slammed and then there was silence. In the morning I went to buy some further bedding, which the boy packed at the back of our buggy. . . . I reckoned that it would cost very little more for six of us to live than for three. The meat cost us nothing, except John's time and ammunition ; nor did the potatoes and other vegetables. Mentally I made a perfectly outrageous profit. In reality, of course, I didn't.

The two little boys were climbing on to the table

in the hotel dining-room while their placid-looking mother finished her meal with a cigarette. She had heard, she said, that the Simba valley was not exactly a healthy place. It was funny, I thought, that she should come by such knowledge down at Nairobi, considering we never heard it mentioned, when we were there. She decided, however, to risk it and went across to Nymba's one and only garage to hire the one and only Ford car available, and arranged to follow me down to the farm the following day. The trip cost her over ten pounds !

Food began to dominate my life. The cook was getting discontented. He did not like to cook for White children, he said, because they did not know what they liked. After my careful description of the discomforts of the house the lady knew exactly what to expect. Luckily she did not seem disappointed, but after the first day or two she became profoundly bored. She also got a swollen face. She lounged in that typical way that most women eventually learn in the tropics. Moodily and languidly she slouched and sagged in my camp-chair, reading the cheaper kind of novels which she had brought with her. Her two little boys were left to themselves and her servant, who incidentally did not like the cook. The children, too, hated Marie at sight and continually teased her. On the third day they bored a hole through the mud wall of the house, a hole big enough to push their heads through. The servant never stopped them. White children were infallible ! Smilingly we repaired the damage which the mother did not seem to have noticed. The following day the children drowned the cook's fourteen newly-hatched chickens which he had lately acquired. After that my cook " forgot " the extra little rice-pudding Percy wanted, and the scrambled eggs that Cyril preferred to boiled eggs.

There was a constant carrier doing the trip to Nymba to fetch those little extras without which such women cannot live. She wanted her liqueur, Benedictine for preference ; she also needed a case of stout to counteract the " thinness " of her blood. " The tropics, you know." Her husband was a shopkeeper ; he could afford it. A glass of stout at lunch-time and a " gin and it " after dinner, a book and a length of pink crêpe-de-chine which she worked into the most seductive under-garments, was the routine of her day. I wondered how her husband managed without her, and if he ever felt the void. Her children developed chicken-pox a fortnight after their arrival and Marie caught it as well a little later. After these unexpected blows the cook also had it and then several *shamba* workers, until it eventually spread up the valley, causing havoc everywhere. Chicken-pox, once it attacks natives, becomes a much more virulent disease than Europeans can realise.

In the end it was the snakes which drove my guest away, a month before she intended to leave. A medium-sized mamba in the sleeve of her dressing-gown decided her to depart. And a few days later the children discovered a puff-adder in a corner of their bedroom. I came upon them just as they were preparing to poke it with a stick. . . . I could not blame my guest for wanting to go for I, too, turned physically sick at the sight of those silent, slow-moving, fumbling things with their forked tails, those seemingly useless inhabitants of an unfriendly earth. I had come across them whilst picking grenadillas or bunches of bananas. Usually I shouted. The terror in my voice always fetched the natives who came armed with sticks, which they had in readiness at all times. With hatred and fury they killed the innocent creature, still lashing at it long after it was dead. The body of the snake would lie wriggling till sunset. . . .

One day a silver-coloured snake about eight feet long came within half a yard of Marie. I saw it first, rushed up to the child and pulled her back— just in time. I yelled with horror until a native came running up carrying a piece of rock, which he threw at the reptile. The snake, frightened and furious, reared into the air ready to strike, missed its victim and suddenly like lightning disappeared into the bush. . . .

It was almost with emotion I saw my guest depart. Soon after sunrise our native groom drove her off to Nymba. I was convinced at that moment that in Kenya even indifferent company was better than none at all. I found, studying my accounts, that I was exactly three pounds to the good over the deal ! I had made three pounds, not counting the damage done. . . .

Almost recklessly John ploughed the land once more, preparing it for a second crop, the first young plants having been eaten by the locusts. Besieged with doubts, as I secretly was, I daily racked my brains for ways and means to save our capital. Once I even wrote to Nairobi, suggesting that in view of the Government grants for land development, it would be advisable to build a railway down the Simba valley ! I did not get an answer. I also wrote to an advertising agent, who wrote glowing weekly articles about places he had visited in Kenya, to come down to Simba and give us an enthusiastic write-up ! Dishonest though my suggestion was, my conscience troubled me not. He wrote a charming letter in reply. He would very much like to come, very much indeed ; but as he was paid to go where he was sent and paid to say what was expected of him, he just could not permit himself the pleasure. He would, however, be very pleased to take me out to dinner, if I happened to be in Nairobi in the near future.

## XXVII

THE FOURTH YEAR WAS DULY CROSSED OFF THE calendar. After that (for over eighteen months) we had not a single drop of rain. The houseboy was busy all day watering a linen-sheet which I hung over the door, which tended to cool the air within. Dawn after dawn broke with the same blue sky overhead. . . .

Another cloud of locusts arrived, but this time the insects could do us no harm for there was nothing for them to destroy. The cloud obscured the sun, growing larger and larger. And then the giant locusts dropped to the ground—there could be no stopping them—and suddenly the sun blazed forth again with an almost uncanny brilliance. Life for a moment ceased to be humdrum. The cook's chickens which had been feeding wearily under the direct rays of the sun, were suddenly blessed with this " manna from heaven." The badly-developed coffee-sapplings were parched and so ignored by the locusts. John did not even cease his ploughing ; he urged the oxen on and on, for all the world like Adam cast out of his Eden. Poor White men, I thought, struggling with eternal anxiety in their hearts, while the negroes with their frugal needs were free to lie in the sun (after they had paid their hut tax, of course) unless they became obsessed with the ambitions to be White men, too.

Sitting down to rest a while, for the way was

steep as I returned from one of those idle walks I
took to keep fit, I honestly wished I were dead. The
enjoyment of the untouched wilderness should have
been mine, as it should also have been John's. The
primitive beauty of the natural forest I had just
returned from should have been a privilege to
behold ; I should have wanted to sing. Was my
enjoyment of things becoming warped by our
tremendous struggle, our anxieties and ill-health ?
Was I, perhaps, blind to the beauty of our valley ?
Was this part of Kenya beautiful after all—as a couple
of holiday-makers, who had called upon us on their
way to Billy's farm the day before, had proclaimed
enthusiastically ?

An elderly gentleman, followed by a very young
wife and a retinue of natives had ridden up our avenue
bordered with huge rocks (which John had carried
there the first month of our arrival, when he was still
desperately ambitious to own a really pretty homestead). The couple had arrived on horse-back.
Heaven knows who had lent them the lovely animals,
which were doomed to die if they were to continue
their voyage down the Simba valley. The lady wore
a thick white veil over her face to protect her skin
from the sun, her husband's portly back and shoulders
were also protected from the sun by pads, lined with
red flannel. He was feeling very hot. They were not
the kind of people one associated with serene philosophy and that capacity for deep contentment one
meets among the humble—yet they raved about the
beauty of the country. " Marvellous, absolutely
marvellous," the girl-wife said, carefully lifting her
veil for a moment.

" The solitude fairly gets you," added the husband,
" doesn't it ? "

They knew Billy's mother and had been in the

country just one week. In the rear their lorry came rumbling along laden with tents and a set of brand new cane chairs. They were going to camp on Billy's place—cane chairs, whisky, cocktail-cabinet and all.

The lady spoke. " We visited Madagascar last week, marvellous place ! Next week we will be off to China—just to see the world, you know, before he . . . before we are too old. A bit hot though, isn't it ? " she added casting her suddenly critical eyes over our farm. Her voice had grown a little patronising. How quickly I had learned to detect that tone of voice !

" Coffee ? " she asked, pointing to the uneven, mangy-looking plantation. " Pays well, doesn't it ? "

" Not too badly, once it bears," I lied bravely.

" Must do," she laughed gaily, " or else no one would stay, would they ? "

" No they wouldn't," I smiled back.

" Heavens, I do feel sticky," she sighed. " I am dying for a bath and to change my undies. I change them three times a day at least. Can't bear feeling sticky, can you ? "

After they had gone I felt that I should have been more hospitable and asked them in, but I had nothing to offer them—not even a " drink," and they were not the sort of people that one asked to have a glass of limejuice, or tea with scones gone stale with slightly rancid butter. I had wanted desperately to be alone, and now being alone once more I seemed to feel more alien to this soil than I had ever felt before ; more alien than the girl on the horse had felt.

To my right someone had driven a post deep into the ground. Billy's boundary. Our oxen had strayed beyond it and had heavily grazed some of his grass. I knew that he did not know of this or else he would have sent a note complaining. He was getting like that, more and more. His chickens, too, had died and the wire-netting of their run was half-buried in the ground, trodden down by cattle. Yes, Billy was the legal owner of this patch of Africa, a thousand acres, the same as we with our thousand acres ; but neither owned them in reality for they remained a wilderness more unyielding than any land Providence has ever given mankind to till.

The cook who had also been for one of his mysterious walks, for he did not walk for walking's own sake, had spotted me sitting alone. This was an opportunity he could not resist in which to air his views. From a respectful distance he shouted across the equivalent of " a nice day." " Things are rotten," he said, and promptly spat. With his right arm he indicated the universe, the cloudless sky, the insects. He then picked up a stick and started to look into the bushes, challenging the snakes which might lurk there, and presently he threw a stone at something or other which I couldn't see.

" *Memsahib*," he said twisting his cap, an appallingly hot cloth-cap which a missionary had once discarded, and which the same missionary had taught him to lift in the presence of White people. " *Memsahib*," he said again, closely examining the inside of his cap, " you must have been wondering many times why I stay here with you in the Simba valley."

" Yes ? " I encouraged him, for that was what he expected me to do.

" What I mean is, it's hot here and no fun much, the women not much to look at. Up there," he pointed vaguely to the east, " where *Bwana* X lives, it is much better. He has an orchard, an orchard," he lied, " as big as your farm. English fruit, White man's food ; apples, plums, lying about like goat's dung. Plenty of music too. Five hundred boys work there," he lied again. " *Bwana* X very much money. He not work. He grand gentleman. He drink, drink all day. *Memsahib*, too. But I like it here," he added after a painful silence, " I like having plenty of meat, meat all day long. I like shoot with *Bwana's* gun like White man. I shoot at other boys, make them run."

He grinned, his eyes bulged more than ever, as he pulled a kind of home-made saxaphone from his baggy trousers. Putting back his cap where it belonged, he pierced the silence with sounds so unmusical and yet so jubilant, that I felt considerably more cheerful. Encouraged by my smile, he blackbottomed down the narrow path, a philosopher, a poet, and a very happy man.

A few yards from where I had been sitting, I saw that at the foot of a tree the ground had been disturbed and carefully covered over again with twigs. The cook had buried his wages, wisely leaving his wife behind to wash his other shirt. Women, he often remarked, need no money. With men it was different; they needed clothes and boots these days, and nice bedding, pocket knives, mirrors. . . . And now he was saving up to buy his first razor and a pair of horn-rimmed glasses. He had shown me the inside of his hut since he had made himself a new bed, of which he was very proud, a sort of hammock of sacking, covered with a straw mattress and two cotton blankets, which his wife washed every week. She herself slept on the floor contentedly. Above the bed, dangling from a string, hung a gaudy print of Jesus on the cross. At the foot of the bed, suspended from the rafters, hung a jam jar filled with dirty water. He dipped his fingers into it, crossed himself and sprinkled his bed with it. He had brought a whisky bottle full of " holy water " from Nymba, but had since had to thin it down, as it dried up so quickly.

Other pictures adorned his walls, for he was very fond of pictures. Covers from *Nash's Magazines* were his favourites. He had bought them from his friend the policeman who had rescued them from his master's the superintendent's wastepaper basket.

# XXVIII

TIME SEEMED ETERNAL, YET THE YEARS PASSED quickly when you did the same thing every day in the same isolated place. Seasons moved without much change. There was always so much for John to fight against, but to me time hung heavily. I thought about many things! Those events which were trivial were those that stood out in the end ; life was never sensational. The stuff of which " thrillers " are made was conspicuously absent. Small incidents, like the cook standing there with his verminous cap in his hands wanting to be friendly ; the sight of a herd of gazelles grazing and then suddenly stampeding as they caught the frightening odour of human-beings ; a young buck, his nostrils quivering, protecting the females. Or again, strangers standing in the doorway ; negroes wanting to work for us because though poor as we were and often paid them less than other people, they knew that we liked them—White people dropping in at sunset ; strangers passing by—these are the scenes one remembered. . . .

It was in March when a stranger waited by the gate, leading a donkey. He was dressed in black except for his helmet, which was white. His face, too, was white, as if he rarely faced the sun. I can still see him standing there in the early morning sun, unshaven, looking ill. As he greeted me, his face lit up in that way that only an Irishman's face lights up when he smiles.

" I hear you have a small daughter," he said, " who has not been baptised yet." His eyes twinkled. He knew I had sinned, sinned in the light of his faith ; but he was ready to absolve me there and then, still holding his donkey by the gate. " I have been sent to baptise her. You will let me baptise her ? " he pleaded, as if appealing to my better nature.

He had ridden his donkey from Nymba and had spent the night in a shelter belonging to a derelict farm whose owner (in despair and yearning for company) had joined the Foreign Legion. The man before me was a holy man and very simple. Father Higgs had once been a great preacher at home, but becoming too popular for his peace of mind, he had turned his back upon the world and was now gravely troubled over such omissions as an unbaptised child. He stayed with us two nights, but he was mostly silent, meditating in his room and writing late into the night, tearing sheet after sheet from his writing block in rapid succession. I think he was glad to be with us ; he dropped into our privacy as if he, too, belonged. His dressing-table was turned into an altar. He had brought with him a coarse white cloth edged with cheap machine-made lace, spreading it over the shabby piece of furniture. And a crucifix and two candles. We had no flowers, for as far as the eye could see into every corner of the valley it would have been impossible to find a single bloom. . . .

He spent much of his time in his " chapel," apparently doing penance for heaven alone knew what. He had brought with him a servant who had followed on foot, who loudly proclaimed the same faith as his master in a most flamboyant kind of way. He wanted to convert the workers in a single night with the sheer power of his enthusiasm. Stolidly the Kikuyu farm-hands sat around him in a circle, just like British working-men being mildly entertained—but completely unmoved ! The Kavirondos who were religious by temperament almost invariably became Mohammedans or Catholics, partly because they could thus label themselves to the rest of the world with public praying and crossing of breasts. They were greatly impressed. The cook fetched his rosary from under his pillow and rubbed it shiny on the sole of his foot ; he also brought a bucket of water to be blessed. He bottled it carefully and by and by sold " portions " to his friends. He sold it quite cheaply, but after an apparently unlimited supply his friends began to get suspicious (and said behind his back) that he was doing the blessing himself. There was a regular pilgrimage from other farms, ending in the usual sing-song, twanging of guitars, shrieking of the cook's panpipes and drinking of tea. Kikuyus went quietly back to their huts, sober and still unbelieving. An old man, slightly puzzled, shook his greying head —but then they did not really care for Kavirondos. . . .

Father Higgs said Mass, and then Marie was duly baptised. Before Mass, the cook had confessed his sins at length, the ones he recognised as such. He stayed longest on his knees, out-kneeling the priest, until the spirit of the ceremony had long fled. He was a showman to the core.

Blessing us, the priest departed two hours before sunset, leaving the place to brood again. The sun was flaming into my eyes as I watched him riding slowly towards the horizon. I had given him the last of my savings—a golden sovereign. A handful of Kavirondos, the cook's guests, were singing loudly, " *Tantum ergum preciosis,*" and then slowly, day by day, their fervour died down. With their inborn fondness for demonstrations, they would make ideal recruits for any political-party requiring the wearing of coloured shirts! Kikuyus being by instinct more reflecting, stood like a race apart. Coldly they appeared to dissect their singing brothers. Like the ancient alchemists, they had more faith in the potency of some concocted powder or the curses of a witch.

# XXIX

W HILST I WORKED IN THE OPEN (NOT THAT I
could do much)—a little weeding in the vegetable-
garden, mostly for the sake of exercise—I soon grew
more alert to sounds. . . . In the solitude of the
spirit, I also frequently re-lived the past ; I heard
the sound of insects, which seemed to multiply as I
listened ; I heard the water splashing over the pebbles
from the stream several hundred yards away. . . .
The usual every-day sounds such as the cracking of a whip, or the cursing of the ploughboy,
or the passing of a neighbour's wagon ceased to
exist, and many fainter sounds crowded into my
consciousness. . . .
Cruel, distressing things are happening around you,
wars between the insects such as destruction between
two species of ants—red ants against black ants ;
small, rapid, intelligent red ants winning the upper-
hand against an army of black ants which are twice
their size and number. . . . A quarrel is also going
on in the maize-field, the tops of the plants are waving
frantically for a second or two—and then silence, a
kind of peace reigns once more. . . . The crunching
of dry earth beneath the naked foot of a native comes
upon my consciousness, and then a letter is handed
to me. . . .
My heart gave a leap of anxiety, for letters were
of the outside world of which I seemed almost to have
grown afraid. I had so few dealings with anyone,

and notes were so often written by cantankerous people who had an unexpected complaint to make. There were two tickets in the letter. A Red-Cross charity-ball had been arranged, to be held at the Grand Hotel in Nymba. The price of the tickets was 30s. The native had walked a long way and these were the last tickets he had left.

I had seen so little of people and once I had been very fond of dancing—but thirty shillings were a fortune to me, and John needed new boots. And yet I suddenly wanted to go ! I hurried down the hill-side to find John, knowing that he would want me to go. . . . Crowds of people would be there, farmers from every quarter of the district, young men and then young women mostly. " You will have to go alone," said John, " but go you must."

I returned to the garden to weed again and thought it over. I had no suitable clothes for a dance. . . . But it was to be fancy dress. That was easier and much cheaper. Excitedly I went to rummage in my bottom-drawer. White petticoats now out of fashion, bits of lace and embroideries, a red shawl and an artificial rose. . . . How red that rose looked in the daylight ! It made everythiing else look dead and faded. . . . These were things of the past, faintly calling me back. What a break in the monotony it would be for me to go to the dance ! Between me and the things in the bottom-drawer there stood several years, but they fell off me in a flash. I was to be young again, and dance !

The second herd-boy drove Marie and me proudly into Nymba a week later. The ground was dry and going was easy, except for the jolting. I already seemed to be feeling better in health. . . . John would not come, partly because of economy and partly because he hated dancing and had at all times but little desire for company. Marie, almost drowned under her pith-helmet, was going to see other White children for once. But she was a quiet child and never spoke unless it was necessary.

My first call as we arrived about tea-time, was to the little private cemetery adjoining the small church. I had a premonition that Father O'Hara was dead. By a brave young pepper-tree lay a few graves, graves of missionaries mostly, and little children : babies, victims of some tropical disease. The same small iron crosses, all in a row ; a few sickly pansies, kept alive by frequent watering ; here and there a wreath made of black and white beads which someone must have sent from home. The wind swept up from the plains, setting up a tinkling sound as it tore at the iron crosses and raised the dust of the neighbourhood. Father O'Hara was not dead. . . . He had been " spared " ; he had gone up to Lake Victoria Nyanza they told me at the hotel, to start yet another mission. Returning to the hotel, I took a short cut through the narrow street of the bazaar. A fine-looking native woman in a heliotrope wrap languidly invited passing natives to come in. She had that " come if you like, and leave it if you don't " attitude of the vamp. The interior of the corrugated-iron hovel was but little better than a farm-hand's hut ; there were no windows, just a doorway with an Indian beaded curtain hanging above it. The shining knobs of an iron-bedstead glittered in the light of a kerosene lamp. Three negroes in the shadowed end of the room were squatting on the floor gambling.

Our herd-boy with a month's wages in his pocket and dressed in his best clothes, came sauntering down towards me. He was going to bank his money, he said, with an Indian shopkeeper who charged him only a small fee for looking after his earnings. It was safer, he thought, than keeping it in his hut ; less trouble than burying it in the ground. He was also going to change his paper-money into silver. Silver did not deteriorate. The Indian, however, asked for twenty-five per cent commission on any money changed. . . . It was worth it, he thought. After all, his savings had been only " paper." It was a blessing, I thought, that by law the natives were not allowed to drink. There was just a chance, though, that he might not reach his banker before he succumbed to the dreary delights of the one street bazaar.

Leaving this odorous huddle of shanties, I went back to the hotel—to my old room with brand new linoleum on the floor ! There was also a creaking iron-bedstead, not as good and not nearly so ornate as the dark woman's of the bazaar appeared to be. The hotel needed brightening up. It was clean, that was all, and still generously disinfected. The aspect of the township was still gloomy ; it would always be gloomy, as it was almost treeless and so many of the houses were mere make-shift shanties. Things looked temporary only . . . no one built as if they really meant to stay.

Marie had met another White girl her own age, and after a moment's silent mutual contemplation she had a sudden shrieking fit of hysterics. I promptly put her to bed where she lay for a long time still trembling. " I want to go home ! " she shrieked again and again. It is hard to realise that the forsaken Simba valley has by force of circumstances become home to someone, my child !

Nymba was busier than usual owing to the ball. Some Union Jacks were nailed up on the wall of the hotel dining-room, and the manager had miraculously produced a few chrysanthenums. A Goanese waiter filled the vases and two boys were polishing the floor with linseed oil. A few young men had also arrived in noisy cars, looking restless, feeling in desperate need to paint the place red. There was not much in Nymba to paint red, for immediately behind the group of houses it was almost a desert of uninhabited, unfertile country. So they lounged lazily instead, stretching themselves out on the same old cane chairs (now much mended with string) and very soon got drunk. The manager stood on the steps of the verandah and suddenly turned out the light. . . . One could just as well get drunk in darkness.

A few women had arrived the day before ; one of them having brought a baby from a place a little down the line. The child was but a few weeks old and the harassed mother was terribly troubled, for the child was ill and showed the same symptoms as one of her other children who had but recently died. Up and down she walked, carrying the little burden, the baby crying weakly all the time. It had cried all day and nothing she did could stop it. Going with her to her room, I took the baby and lay down on the other bed with the little creature lying face downwards on my chest. It suddenly fell asleep. I dared not move. Presently the mother also fell asleep, but the baby only slept two hours, when it began to wail again, waking its mother, who started once more her soothing journey up and down, up and down. . . .

The young men on the verandah had now reached that perfect state of drunken ecstasy which is recognisable by a look of complete happiness and the absence of all intelligence.

After a terribly close night and an equally drowsy morning, the rest of the guests arrived from the outskirts. In the hotel-yard, where the Indian *dhoby* had spread out some very much " blued " hotel sheets to dry, one car after another arrived. By four o'clock there was not one car in that yard which would have fetched more than ten pounds in England ! A few old-timers and those living further afield, arrived by buggy.

The ball had begun. . . . A native band coached with infinite patience by an English band-master, playing entirely without music with the most perfect rhythm, tuned up for a foxtrot. Everybody was there, even the railway people and the smaller shop-keepers who behaved with great dignity and decorum. Most of the young men were still in the bar—a filthy little place, filled with men who aired their feelings by peppering their talk with oaths. I caught a glimpse of one of the young fellows who had been drinking stolidly for two days, leaning heavily on the counter, his blood-shot eyes looking dejectedly at an emaciated goat which he held on a string. Dressed in a white sheet, he was supposed to represent Gandhi.

" This place is dead," he said at frequent intervals, addressing the goat. " We are all dead, Nanny," he insisted. " Nanny, this place has died on us."

The wife of the magistrate danced sedately with the permanent-way inspector ; the magistrate, an old man now, would soon be hopelessly drunk and become noisy. Freddie, back once more, walked in with his latest lady friend, a woman exquisitely dressed as an eastern dancer. He himself wore the clothes of a curate, flat hat and all. It suited him almost too well. A tall woman who had once been on the stage, gave an exhibition dance, a *danse du ventre*, which looked anything but seductive as she was the kind of woman who would have looked much better on the golf-course. The negroes of the band gaped.

The White man's *ngoma* (dance) appeared to them ridiculous.

The man with the goat was crying now. . . . The goat seemed equally unhappy as it stood with its hind leg in the spittoon trembling violently. Someone tried to make her drunk as well by giving her bread soaked in whisky—but she bravely refused to open her mouth.

Soon there were about a hundred people there, and I had my programme full. Those who were sober, danced ; others tried, but gave it up ; others again suggested a moonlight walk or a drive into some desolate spot on the Simba road in a rickety car. The doctor dropped in for a dance with me. He was noticeably out of condition and wheezed and panted a great deal. " The baby in number seven is gravely ill," he said as he regained his breath, and then he went out again. The manager of the Grand Hotel who had been sitting in a corner by himself smoking a burned-out old pipe came up and asked for a one-step, still balancing his pipe at the end of his teeth. The room divided itself into two camps. On one side sat the members of the club ; and on the other side the would-be-but-could-not-be members. They were being patronised—slightly. I wondered why they had come. The bank manager, a cheerful likeable man, went across the floor and danced with the greengrocer's wife and made her very happy. The District Commissioner and a veterinary-surgeon spoke indefinitely about gardening. They had both tried very hard, and up to a point had succeeded, in producing quite decent gardens which were the pride of Nymba.

During supper the magistrate who sat next to me related many interesting experiences of his varied life. As supper went on, his reminiscences grew increasingly interesting and confidential, until they reached the state when they were merely confidential without being interesting. Decorum gradually fled ; the club members grew less patronising. Presently they hardly cared who was who. Alcohol, I reflected, was also a great leveller. From the bar came a terrific clatter of broken glass and then the goat appeared forlornly by the ballroom door and hid herself behind the band. The odour of natives was preferable to the poor creature than the reek of the bar !

Just after midnight I went to bed. Everyone else was still dancing, but the far-end of the hotel was deserted. From my window I could see the ancient hills of Africa outlined in the moonlight. A sombre background they made to a ghostly little township. The scene looked artificial somehow—like the painting on an oriental screen. There was no sound from the room next door, so the baby was sleeping at last. . . . Freddie had long since gone to look at the moon with his friend, and the magistrate was being led home with a great deal of persuasion by the manager of a trading-company. The old man did not want to go home. . . .

"Don't want to go home," he kept repeating loudly. "Want to say good-night to Mrs. Z, the little b——."

I had had my dance. It had been fun up to a point, but I was ready to go back to the farm. I had lost touch a little with frivolous things, and it struck me that I had grown a little heavy-hearted. Pioneering had done that. . . . There were places in Kenya that brooded evil and such a place was our valley. The misery of that bush country ! One wanted to draw the blinds and turn one's back to its unadulterated sameness. One could not even grumble in a healthy sort of way—no one grumbled unless they were drunk. Complaining, even moderately, was *taboo*. Who wanted another fellow to convince you of your own fears ? After all, we had all " made our beds," and it was only decent to lie on them without grumbling or to get out without a fuss.

Nymba's only taxi fetched the lady in the room next door at dawn. A man, probably her husband, carried the baby. The child was dead. . . .

The European mail which had just come in brought me a very much-belated Christmas calendar, portraying a pine tree heavily laden with snow. Some aunt or other had probably remembered us on Christmas Eve, and had forgotten to write her name on it. All I could detect was " 5d, " pencilled in the left-hand corner. Someone, anyway, wished us a prosperous new year. Prosperous indeed ! The irony of those Christmas wishes ! I had a creeping feeling that slowly, but surely, I was becoming a Socialist.

Another " tough guy " of a pioneer, one of the ecstatic drinkers, felt his way along to the hotel verandah, the most popular meeting-place in Nymba. He had a black eye which was completely closed. His friend and boon-companion followed behind with a lower lip which was cut and swollen ; war-scars which somehow accentuated the expression of puzzled vacancy in his youthful face. The two of them had had a fight soon after the dance had opened, over a girl—one of the few single girls who lived within a day's calling-distance of either of their farms. They had, after the bar had closed, suddenly and unaccountably decided to walk down to the lake together to talk philosophy perhaps, or merely to " have it out " under the moon. On their journey down they were inspired to tear up everything that could be loosened ; a gate here, a post there—by way of protesting against existing conditions. After that, they had steered their way to a little stone shelter which someone in romantic mood had erected years ago, but which was now only used by natives for less romantic purposes. There they sat, blearily looking over the moonlit water, the lake which was so surprisingly level with the ground that it looked like a hole in the earth, a gigantic puddle. Except for the stone shelter the surroundings were uninhabited and deserted for half a mile. The aspect of the place was gloomy and as the night advanced the two friends grew angrier and angrier until eventually they fought. . . .

Apart from the Hindu stores in town, there was now a magnificent grocery-shop owned by a go-ahead White man. In the ironmongery department, behind buckets and brooms, hung several gentlemen's suits suspended from the ceiling. They had been good suits once but were now marked forty-five shillings each. In order to compete with the Indian shop-keepers he too had been forced to give long-term credit to everyone. There had been numerous cases of a fellow going home on leave who could not pay his grocer's bill before departing ; that is, he could not pay and go home as well. He therefore preferred to leave his suits in lieu of payment and the place had thus assumed a slightly pawnshop-ish aspect. The young grocer had brought his aged parents out with him from somewhere in the heart of Gloucester-shire. Transplanted towards the end of the journey of his life, the old man pottered about the shop, swept the floor, packed up parcels and looked unspeakably resigned. His equally old little wife did the housework, alone. They had no servants. I wondered how much longer either of them would be able to stand the physical strain of a life in the tropics. . . .

After I had bought a few necessities, the young man took me through a back door and showed me his lending-library. He had brought it from England, boxes and boxes full of second-hand books. His father had chosen them for him, book by book, and he considered them the very essence of English literature. They were, however, far above the requirements of young fellows who merely yearned for a good yarn. The books were incredibly dirty. There was an old edition of the *Anatomy of Melancholy*, as well as the essays of Montaigne, a few German philosophers and depressing Russian tomes. In fact, nearly all the books were of a serious nature—even his novels.

" For years," began the old man as he came up to me broom in hand, " I have had no other wish in life except to be left alone to read . . . yes, madam, you would not believe it, but there are three thousand books on these here shelves, and I have read every one of them—many of them more than once. I'd grown that self-centred, you wouldn't believe it. Fairly indulgent I was. I don't read now, haven't read a book for nearly a year. There ain't nothing new for me to read anymore. I walks out every Sunday on to that there crater, or I brush the store with only my thoughts for company. It's enough for me. See there," he pointed to the cone-shaped crater to the west, " you'd say that's ugly and bare, now wouldn't you? What is outside of me is nought to me now. It don't matter much where you are, it is what you have got inside you that counts. I am me own philosopher now. Didn't know it, till I had done with reading."

" Here, Pop," called his son, " lend me a hand ! "

After a while he came back and resumed his conversation.

" When I was young I talked and talked, and then, as I said, I read. Heavens, how I read ! And now I'm living my life at last." The old man rambled on.

# XXX

I STOWED MY PARCELS IN THE BUGGY, AND AFTER this break in the tedium of life we drove back into the heart of the valley again. It took us five hours, stopping once or twice by a river to have a drink. The languor of the afternoon affected the mules, which meandered along as if asleep. After the first half-hour's riding, we came to the top of a rise from where we had the last glimpse of Nymba. It looked the kind of little town people built hastily—people who were in a desperate hurry after gold.

Three tall Somalis in russet-brown flowing robes, leading a tiny donkey, came over the horizon, dust rising beneath their sandals. They looked gigantic against the sea of blue behind them and reminded me of the pictures one sees in illustrated Bibles. They appeared to belong to this background and gave it life. They gave it, too, the only touch of colour I came across on the journey. (Oh, how one longed for colour at times!) The Somalis' usual indifference to surroundings was almost superb, for although they can hardly have met a soul for hours and had to step aside to let us pass, they never even glanced at us. They were praying. Amber beads dangled from their lean long hands, and their minds seemed to be on eternal things, but—who knows?—for they are in the main a calculating tribe. . . .

Later on we passed a farm-cart which had turned-turtle at the side of the road. Two disconsolate natives were sitting on the upturned wagon, arguing loudly. Sacks of sweet potatoes and carrots were strewn on the ground and the couple of oxen had walked off to graze. We stopped. Karanga, my driver, had started an excited conversation with the boys long before we got near them. How these natives conversed, their voices travelling high above the din of carriage-wheels ! After a lengthy struggle, the three of them lifted the cart on its wheels again and gravely viewed the damage. They were afraid to go home, they said, their master never listened to " palaver " (explanations). He just used his fists, or else—which was worse—made them pay for the damage out of their wages. For a while they debated with Karanga whether it would not perhaps be best for them to run away. But then arose the question of a *barua* (references), without which they would surely be suspected of some shady misdeed.

Ah, it was sometimes not easy to please White men. They were told to make room for White people when on the road, and if they didn't there was trouble. A motor-car had approached and had used the whole road. There was a ditch on their side, and they promptly turned over into it. . . . It was fate ; didn't we think it was fate ? That was the only explanation, unless it was the White man's fault. In the end they generously decided that, indeed, it had been fate. Definite on that point, they eventually heaved the sacks on to the cart and collected the oxen, gesticulating and talking all the time. They were still talking to Karanga when we had gone out of ordinary hearing-distance ! They had made up their minds to return not because they wanted to in the least, but even an African knows that to do the right thing is usually the easiest in the end.

It was Saturday afternoon, and many natives had

a half-day holiday. Dressed in their unbecoming Sunday best, we met them on their way to visit friends. They shouted to Karanga, asking him to persuade me to give them a lift. There was no room in our " gharry," as the natives called it, what with Marie on my knee and a trunk at the back, as well as the driver at my side who seemed to need a great deal of space for his elbows. On top of the trunk behind, tied in a basket, was a present for Marie—a tabby cat. The only White butcher who had recently come to Nymba to start a business of his own had given it to me. He had been at the dance and we met during a Paul Jones. The man told me modestly that he had been a ship's cook for years, until he had wearied of the job and he and the ship's cat got off at Mombasa to start a new life together. The cat, once she had left the monastic life of the ship, had in due time given birth to seven kittens. The butcher hadn't the heart to kill them, and knowing I had a little girl, he handed me the pussy over the counter together with a joint of beef which I had extravagantly bought for a treat. We had not eaten beef for months and the lean meat of venison loses all attraction if eaten frequently. The cat became a great companion, being very intelligent and full of fun, and was almost as playful as a dog.

One day to our sorrow, however, she suddenly disappeared, apparently for good. Months later the cook swore that he had seen her, looking like a shadow, returning in the dark to sneak into the kitchen. She had looked for food and had run off again into the night. It was the same cat, he said, yet not the same. Some magic had gone into her for she did not even know him any more ; he who had so lovingly fed her ! Every night he poured milk into a saucer, and every morning it had been drunk, until one morning we found her lying on a sack under the kitchen table with five kittens by her side. But as the cook had said, she was never the same again : there was a wild look in her eyes and she had forgotten how to purr. Her kittens were fierce, spitting with such savagery that it seemed the most natural thing for them to leave their shelter at the earliest opportunity and follow their mother, who henceforth disappeared for good. The influence of thousands of generations of purring house-cats had been of no avail—she had " gone native."

I had a pleasant surprise after my return, for John had, with the help of two boys, built a bathroom in my absence, knocking a doorway into our bedroom wall. There were two steps leading elegantly into this new addition to a tiny little homestead. The floor was ten feet by twelve and actually made of wooden planks which he had bought from Bill. The walls were made of daub and wattle. It was by far the nicest room of our house. The bath as well as the water had still to be carried in and out through the door, but we were used to that. One did not linger in one's bath, for it was small, one half of the body having to remain outside while the other half was submerged. I often dreamt of hot water from a tap trickling pleasantly into a scented marble bath. . . . How childish one's day-dreams sometimes became !

The hot wind which was typical of the valley still blew maliciously. The hot air which rose from the depths of the Simba vale created a kind of suction, a vacuum which filled itself rapidly by the cooler air from the plateau above, causing this everlasting wind to blow which roared down into the furnace of Lake Baringo, that notorious ante-room to hell. It was quite different to the much more temperate wind—

the monsoon—which only blew at certain times and promised rain, but didn't always bring it.

Some of the hot nights were eerie indeed, possibly because wild beasts were driven nearer to the places where there was a stream. Perhaps, too, it was the wind which carried the voices of animals to our ears, or it may have been the mating season of hyenas and jackals. Their horrible mocking laughter was as uncanny and melancholy as the singing of our cook who incidentally was a great singer and could keep it up for hours at a non-stop rate. The melody, or the lack thereof, was essentially oriental—a long-drawn, high-pitched note travelling far into the distance (then a few meagre twangs on his primitive guitar) followed by a succession of low notes sung plaintively like an age-old lament. I never grew accustomed to his singing. I wanted to get away from it, to shut it out. Pioneers, I reminded myself, should not be so easily affected. After all, the cook was thoroughly enjoying himself and was completely oblivious of the fact that his happy singing conjured up a sense of loneliness almost unendurable to a stranger to his country.

There was one thing which I taught the natives which they should have known. That was a knowledge of herbs. Higher up on the plateau there grew herbs which Providence must have intended for some special purpose. There was fern of every kind in the woods, from maidenhair to the giant variety, which could either be infused as tea or else used as stuffing for mattresses. It was a cure for stomach trouble and rheumatism as well as a deterrent against bugs. There was wild garlic which could be used internally as well as externally for numerous ailments. There were plantain, wild geranium—which once a year produced a very pale purplish bloom—and many other ferns. But the natives were not interested. They had more faith, I found, in white or pink tablets which White people kept in store against every ailment under the sun than in the curative powers of " mere grass." . . .

It happened that some of our workers, particularly the Kavirondos, asked for an advance in their wages. It was difficult to guess what they did with their pay, for as far as we knew there was no occasion for them to spend their money. It had, too, struck me that the cook had been very silent of late ; no sound came from his hut at night. His child-wife sat by the fire-light, completely naked, crooning to herself, rocking one of Marie's dolls in her arms, perhaps praying to have her wish for a child fulfilled.

" Where is your man ? " I asked her. She quickly put the doll aside and replied : " He playing game with Mesungu, far away, over there." She pointed to the west, where Smith-Smythe, whom we had not seen for a long time, had pitched his tent.

" What kind of game ? " I asked her. " Game like a gharry, that goes round and round, playing with lots of rupees."

On the following day I saw the cook coming hurriedly from the wood. I knew he had been to his savings-bank beneath the tree and I also knew that he had not hidden more money there.

" Where did you go last night ? " I asked him rather sternly.

" Me have game with White man, fine game," he rolled his eyes and clicked his tongue. " Me win money first, and now me lose money. To-morrow me win again, me soon win all the time."

Playing roulette had captivated his soul, for the natives are born gamblers. Not that they had much to lose, but one could not be sure where the habit might lead them. Smith-Smythe had not much to lose either, but every chance to win.

John forbade the cook and the others to go, but a night or two later as I went to bed I saw the cook standing outside our bedroom-window, waiting until the light was turned out when he raced over the fields to the west, to have yet another game. It was not long before he was broke, his savings-bank dug up and left bare. Much sobered, he stayed at home to start saving once more. . . .

# XXXI

JOHN AND I HAD ALREADY GONE TO BED WHEN WE noticed through the open window outlined in the silver light of the moon that someone, a man, was groping his way on to our verandah. For a moment he stood in the gateway, and then there was a knock on the door. A White man's voice called loudly : "Is anyone there?" It was a nice voice—somehow I felt that I had heard it before. John lit the kerosene lamp and in his pyjamas went out, I following in my dressing-gown. The man's fair hair shone in the moon like a halo. He carried an enormous knapsack, a battered topee, a gun and a stick. He was tall, and his clothes were torn as if he had been mauled by a leopard. "Hello," he said, "I see you don't remember me." John held the lamp to his face, and still we did not know him. Leading the way into the sitting-room John lit the lamp.

The stranger burst out laughing. "Don't you remember Peter ; Peter from the boat?" At last we could place him. . . . He was a young man who had come out on the same boat as us ; rather a serious young man who had travelled third-class and would have gladly gone fourth, had there been one. He had spoken to us across the railing for many an hour and we had since often wondered what had happened to him, for he had been tremendously enthusiastic having, I remembered, left a girl at home whom he was going to send for at the earliest opportunity. It

all came back to me in a flash. . . . Peter standing
by the railing looking hungrily across to the other
deck, yearning to join in with other young people of
his class, yet having to share a cabin and a tiny deck
with people who were difficult to talk to.

" Pah ! who but an Englishman wants to bury
money in a new country, a place where there is no
money ? " a young Jew had said to him, leaning non-
chalantly by the rail. I still remember how furious
Peter had been, how white his knuckles were as he
gripped the iron rail. We were just passing Malta
which dazzled in the sunlight, and a happy breeze
from shore had carried with it the sound of church
bells. For a few moments the Jew had made us
think. . . . He had innocently done something unforgivable : he had conjured up a momentary doubt
in our hearts, and Peter very nearly struck him. Peter
was leaning over the rail, while the Jew happily
flicked the ash from his cigarette. He had gone
off at Port Said, confidently waving his bowler hat
to us.

Here was Peter whom we were hardly able to
recognise, whom we would not have known again
had we met him elsewhere ! His cheeks were sunken
and he looked quite old. I hastily fetched some sheets
to make up the spare bed, while John rummaged in
the sideboard for some food, for the cook had long
gone to bed.

" I have turned hobo," Peter said with a laugh,
lifting up his arms to show us a couple of sleeves
hanging loosely from the arm-holes. " I have been
hobo-ing for seven months now, looking for work."

He had once felt so sure of things, as well as of
himself—indeed, much surer than I. How completely Africa had captured his imagination at that
time ! Happily he used to watch the sports on the

second-class deck and clap his hands with the rest of us. There had been no room on his deck for any games, but as he was firmly determined not to break into his £500 which his mother had loaned him in order to give him a chance in a " coming country," he refused to spend any money on second-class comforts. He was not sure at the time what he was going to do with his money. At all costs he was going to keep it safe. . . .

I looked at him, and when he looked up I turned my face away, for I could have wept. He knew how I felt, and there was a moment's silence. " What have you been doing with yourself? " asked John at last.

" You mean, since I was toying with the idea of getting rich quick ? " Peter laughed, as he cut himself a second piece of bread. Not until he had finished his supper did he tell us about his life in Kenya. We urged him to go to bed, but he had badly wanted to talk. . . . It was already past midnight yet we felt that " talking it out " would do the boy good. He told us his story right from the beginning. . . .

As soon as Peter arrived in Nairobi he bought himself a tent, a bed and cooking utensils. Pitching his tent outside the town on a bare patch of land, he then set to without wasting time to look for work. He did not want to do anything rash with his capital before he had learnt to know something of the country. But work was scarce. At the back of his mind he hoped for a partnership in a little business, but there was nothing suitable to justify his risking his mother's savings. Time passed quickly, but in the meantime he had to live. There were, too, other young fellows looking for work ; chaps who stood about in bars, whiling away their time in drink, hoping and hoping for something to turn up. Eventually Peter went up country and started to walk inland, calling on farmers for work. He had had many temporary jobs—of a kind—and so had picked up a fair knowledge of farming. At one place he managed a full-grown coffee-plantation during the owner's absence in England, and was given the run of the absent owner's house with board and lodging and the use of two servants—but there was no pay. But a drought came and the crop was poor. When the owner returned he blamed his manager for his meagre harvest and accused him of ignorance. And he promptly gave Peter the sack.

After two months of idleness the boy got a job during the busy season on a big estate in the highlands, where he mostly drove a tractor and where, incidentally, he had to queue up with the natives to get his wages. Food he had to find himself. On Sundays he would go out with his gun into the bush and try to bag something. . . . It was a very lonely sort of existence but that, too, came to an end. The next two months Peter had spent in hospital, sick with dysentery. After he had got his discharge he took the plunge and bought himself a tiny stretch of land in a valley similar to ours. It was a small slice of land—only three hundred acres all told—which the owner sold in order to raise some necessary funds. Peter's " estate " was a level piece of ground at the edge of a stream, and his neighbour hired him his plough and oxen and then he planted maize, the safest crop in Kenya.

That particular year there had been too much rain—it had rained incessantly—and the place rapidly turned into a swamp. The plants shot up, they were a lovely green. It was a joy to see. Still it rained, until his crop stood deep in water. He had needed tools, several workmen, groceries, gumboots and many other necessaries. But by now there was little money left in the bank, and his crop slowly rotted. . . . The stems of his plants were hollow.

Peter left the valley and his little farm, and found a job with a Dutchman who engaged him more for his company than for the work he could do.

"Poor devil," said Peter. "That Dutchman was as poor as myself." But all Peter had to eat was *posho* (maize meal), whilst his tent had rotted and for seven months he slept in a wagon in the open, under a sheet of tarpaulin. . . .

The talk had done Peter good; but it was two o'clock before we turned in. His girl, he said to me in the dark on the verandah, had got tired of waiting and had married someone else. . . .

Peter was up again at dawn and strolled round the farm. We did not tell him of our own experiences; nor did he ask. The farm told its own story. He knew.

When he returned at breakfast-time, he examined our "crofter's cottage" homestead: low, small windows pierced through a thick whitewashed mud wall, but too dark within to read, even in the day-time. The dresser standing crookedly at one end, and the table at the other. There was also a book-shelf which John had made, which was now filled with an accumulation of books which had been sent out to us by our parents. (They were a strange assortment representing the taste of each individual sender.) The corrugated-iron roof had long been covered with thatch in order to keep out the heat of the sun. Each of the three rooms led straight out into the open. Barely had one left the bed than one stepped out into the wide world, so to speak. Occa-sionally pigs or fowls strayed on to the doorstep, or one of the mules came nibbling at the white linen hanging on the line to dry. Our walls were adorned with countless photographs, parting gifts of people by whom we were now long forgotten, which were gradually being eaten by the most minute insects quite invisible to the naked eye. Some of the faces had already completely disappeared. . . .

Peter picked up a scythe and started to cut the tough grass outside his bedroom door, still wet with morning dew. In the meantime the houseboy was mending his coat, after a fashion. He was very proud of wielding the needle and always expected much praise. Peter urged him to cut the sleeves off altogether, but Karioki would not hear of it. " White men," he said horrified, " must have sleeves." Later, Peter went and bagged a guinea-fowl which we had for dinner. It was very stringy—but they usually were. After dinner, feeling completely rested he talked.

" There's one thing this blooming country has given me, that is a damned sight more philosophy than is good for a young chap. . . . Gives you a sense of humour, too—if you let it. Those ruddy propagandists at home," he went on after a smoke, " trying to rearrange the scheme of things, wanting to populate the distant places of the Empire, trying to relieve the pressure at home at all costs—if ever I come across one of them, I'll wring his neck ! But seriously," he continued, " the change of things, of conditions, is terriffic. Old doddering So-and-so at home is still staggering from the effects. It's not their fault," he went on more generously. " All they can do at their age is to look back. Someone's always being sacrificed first before the old opinions change. Habit, loyalty, the good old disorder of things ! " Peter was a good talker when in the mood, and he dearly loved an audience.

" Doing justice to all people, what a mess it is getting them into at home," put in John, defending the old regime.

" The chances for young men in the future don't lie in grubbing for food in hellish outposts of a weary Empire," said Peter. " It's in science. There is no limit in that direction."

" What will we do," asked John, " without some of the old traditions ? "

" Traditions be hanged, ; there is no guarantee behind them ! If I had my way I'd dig up the whole of England, give each man a cow, a pig or two and a spade, and teach them to grub in their own soil. I'd give them cheap beer, cheap tobacco and teach them to sing the old folk-songs again and the jolly old country dances. I'd want them to have the kind of life which has some permanency, not this sort of aimless come-to-day-and-go-to-morrow existence. Some of them are beginning to realise at last that they can't arrange the scheme of things by encouraging emigration. You can't regulate things like that, that blooming myth is exploded. Once this valuable career of mine is over, and if I ever see the Old Country again, I'll join the Air Force or the Army, if they'll have me. Gosh," he sighed, " I wish there was another war ! "

After this bout of talking Peter relapsed into silence, lying happily in my deck-chair. He did not want to go back to bed. He could not sleep, he said. " What if I turned native ? " he went on after breakfast, sadly contemplating his boots which had now become useless. . . " Go through a ceremony of marriage with a *bibi* and then lie in the sun for evermore, *dolce far niente* for the rest of my life, glamorous, passionate and carefree ! There's one thing about this place, it is always warm."

There was an old pair of white tennis-shoes which John had occasionally worn of an evening, which I gave Peter as a parting gift before he went up to the plateau, hoping to find a job on one of those enormous estates which were situated some thirty miles to the east of us. The shoes would hardly last him a day ; but they were all I had to give him. He had not even wanted to take them, and the whole of the afternoon was spent trying to patch his old ones with bits of zebra-hide.

" Come back and see us again soon ! " I called after him as he climbed the hill. Casting his doubts once more to the winds he waved his hat to me, giving me three hearty cheers which echoed in the valley.

We never heard of or saw him again. . . .

## XXXII

THE COOK TOOK TWO DAYS' LEAVE AS SOON AS HE had received his first month's wages after he had lost his little fortune. He returned punctually as usual and was heavily laden. I saw him coming in the distance, as I looked down the road—that road which somehow ought to have brought something unexpected every day, but which, alas, so rarely did. There was not a merciful scrap of cloud in the sky, and the cook had walked fifty miles. He was covered with the ashes of miles of burnt-out grass through which he had come. The wind, too, had sent volumes of ashes skywards, covering nature with a grey-black shroud. It was the kind of hideous outlook which deprived a fellow of the last vestige of enthusiasm, but I am glad to say that it never affected the cook in that way! There is much to be said for a cook as insensitive as he was!

He had bought a crate of chickens to add to those he already possessed. I usually bought his eggs, so did Bill occasionally, and sometimes—as a treat— we had one of his fowls for dinner. Trailing behind him on a leash was a dog—the most melancholy dog I had ever come across. Removing the crate from his woolly head, he introduced me proudly to his animal. " This is Simba " (lion), he said, pulling the frightened creature closer. " I always wanted a dog," he grinned. He seemed inordinately proud of it. He had bought the creature from his friend

the policeman. It had cost him five shillings, " only."
The policeman, who had been given two shillings by a
White man to lead the mongrel away and shoot him,
had not done so badly over the deal. The dog,
wretched animal though he was, seemed to add a
sort of indefinable dignity to the cook's position.

The chickens were let loose in the compound
behind the house where the cook had his hut, and
the dog was relieved of the ticks which he had collected
on the way—I hoped in vain that the cook would
wash his hands before preparing our dinner. . . .

Simba was never playful or even moderately happy.
Whatever one's speculations regarding incarnation, it
was clear that Simba did not possess the soul of a
dog. Being a very serious animal, he had no sense of
humour. In that, perhaps, he was almost human ;
the kind of creature which makes no friends, having
lived for years in solitude. He was, I noticed upon
closer inspection, riddled with fleas, but that did not
worry him unduly or else he had not the spirit to
scratch. The cook spoke sharply to Simba (it suited
him well to order something about), but the poor
animal was altogether too deferential. Simba was
transparently thin, a mere framework with a length
of mangy skin stretched tightly across him. He had
a thin, very long tail which he wore curled into a
downward drooping knot. No one ever saw him
wag it, nor did it even uncurl. . . . He came to a
bad end though, as a creature like Simba somehow
would. A leopard mercifully ended his misery, as
he lay in the hut one night with his head pushed
through the gap in the straw, probably trying to get
a breath of air. Suddenly and without warning,
Simba was snatched from the bosom of his family,
and quietly and without a fuss he gave up his
weary ghost.

One Sunday morning, rather later than usual, we had our breakfast out of doors under the overhanging iron roof, when the cook's chickens, one by one, came trooping round the corner of the house as usual looking for crumbs. Their appearance was shocking : the cook had plucked them, half-way up ! Like French poodles, their hind-quarters were bare. The birds looked hardly decent. They were, however, completely unselfconscious as they grubbed happily about, quarrelling and pecking crumbs off the coco-matting. There were several dozen of them, and all but the cockerel were thus deprived of their feathers.

With much swaggering, the cook came round to explain. He knew we would think it strange, if not cruel.

" I thought," he said, " that I knew all about chickens, but now I learn more." It had been a toilsome, laborious task, plucking live chickens, requiring a great deal of patience. He had sat up all night to do it, but, " no doubt I will be paid for my trouble. You see, they will lay many eggs now and much easier." He had barely said these words when two of the hens began to cackle over by the store house. Frantic excitement ! " Listen," said the cook, " one egg, two eggs ! " Within an hour there were two more and by evening we had a dozen. The output had been trebled at first, but then it began to drop, falling as low as six eggs by the end of the week. Yet the cook solemnly stuck to the advice which he had been given by his friend that the " de-feathering " would prove good in the end—and strangely enough—it did !

About this time a youngish man and his wife and little daughter built themselves a house some four miles to the north of us. They arrived one Friday afternoon in an ancient Morris Oxford,

followed later by a wagon loaded with implements.
Our new neighbour, a lanky fellow, already getting
bald, had once been a clerk. He looked a clerk and
he remained a clerk, temperamentally and physically.
He had now invested all his money in the same sort
of fools' paradise as ours—but did not as yet know
it. I came upon him sitting on a rock, scratching
his head and contemplating the numerous parts of
a plough, which lay spread out in front of him.
Like a jigsaw puzzle, it seemed completely to absorb
him. Through his previous occupation as a bank
clerk, he heard that the value of our land was going
up owing to " growing demand " and its splendid
coffee-producing qualities. So he threw up his job,
rushed down the valley and hurredly bought a
thousand acres. Coffee it was going to be. . . . All
that was wanted now was rain. In the meanwhile
he had to put his plough together, but he did not
find it easy, for the native, he said, had lost the
illustrated instructions which came with the plough !

After a month or so, I walked the four miles to
the three-roomed wooden house which had been
erected by Indian carpenters before our neighbours
arrived, and found the lady of the house sitting on the
verandah knitting contentedly, while her young
daughter played in the shade of the dining-room. The
little girl was not allowed out of doors till five o'clock,
as she invariably got sunstroke. The child therefore
had exactly an hour before sunset in which she could go
for a walk, or frolic on her father's parched estate.
Her name was Fay—the very name for her. She
looked as though she might at any moment fade
away into some fairyland, so white and angelical
was her lovely little face. Playing by herself, she had
a horde of imaginary friends and it looked as though
she really saw them. Poor little Fay, leading an

entirely imaginary life while her father and mother were going to make a fortune for her. Strange though it may seem, Fay never took an interest in Marie, her imaginary friends having grown infinitely more real to her. Indeed, real flesh and blood seemed to frighten the little girl.

Her mother, as so often is the case, was the very opposite to her child. She was a shockingly conventional woman to have ventured out into such an unconventional world. She had all the silver and cut-glass of a lifetime on her mirrored sideboard, plush chairs and other blue plush comforts. She was also very prim and proper, the product of a cathedral town. I shuddered to think what might happen if the Scotch woman were to call on her.

" My grandfather the Bishop," she ventured, " my uncle the Dean, and my brother the Deacon. . . ." As I had no one much to boast about in our family and I had for years lived too close to the realities of life to find her values interesting, we did not cultivate a close acquaintanceship. Even the wilds, it seemed, the common dangers and hardships, fears and failures of humanity, do not make the whole world kin.

It was two months later when my houseboy gravely came to tell me that the *memsahib* of the " man with the bald patch " had *saa-mbia* (born badly) ; in other words, had had a miscarriage. How the native knew was a mystery to me, for White people do not confide in them ; yet, not unlike servants at home, they seemed to know everything which concerned their masters. They had a habit of peeping, especially at night. A gap in the curtains to them was as good as going to the pictures.

I promptly went to see Mrs. Y, and found her sitting up in bed, placidly knitting. Fay was dressed up in her mother's wedding-veil and was giving an exhibition dance to an invisible audience, for whom she had placed all the chairs in a circle. Overcome by weakness, her mother suddenly burst into tears. My heart involuntarily went out to her, seeing her thus humanised.

" Who knows," I said, trying to comfort her and thinking of the miserable life a child was forced to live under such circumstances, " perhaps it's for the best."

She stopped crying at once and drying her tears turned to me wide-eyed and reproached : " Oh, how can you say such a thing ? "

Feeling rather brutal, I left her mourning something which she had not as yet known. . . . That the still-born child had been spared a lonely, unhealthy existence never entered her head. She was not that sort of woman. As a whole, I thought, I preferred the Scotch woman. It seemed more honest, and just as well under the circumstances when living alone to call a spade a spade. . . .

Passing the shed where her husband's plough stood (and which John had helped him to assemble), I came upon one of their *shamba* boys, airing his goods and chattels in the sun. Amongst a litter of straw and sacking, I recognised several pieces of my own household linen which had disappeared at odd intervals ; there was also an old enamel chamber-pot, in which he cooked his *posho*. Blissfully unaware of its former purpose, he proudly stirred his porridge. He sang. His needs were few and easily satisfied. I let him be, although I could have claimed my initialled belongings. His *memsahib*, though, might have been upset. Natives, as in this case, if they stole at all, usually stole from their neighbours and rarely from their employers.

I passed our few remaining farm-hands, who had spent about three months uprooting a few dozen tree-stumps—but there was little to show for their labour. One year, two years, three years in the bush, how little seemed to have been achieved, and yet how much ! I also met Bill on the way, leaning disconsolately against a tree, chewing a blade of grass, his ancient gun which had once been his father's slung over his shoulder. He was out to get some meat to give to his ever-hungry dogs. Bill, too, had a merry little streamlet running through the middle of his thousand acres and at the moment he was attempting to irrigate his vegetable-patch as well as his half-acre or so of coffee. Yet he might as well have given up the attempt, for the good it did. The water did not get very far, and gradually lost itself trickling down the ruts. Having to face realities had changed Bill even more than it had John ; he had grown rather bitter and was now given to brooding. There was simply not enough for him to do ; and whenever I came across him he seemed to be communing with himself, leaning here and there or squatting on the ground.

It may perhaps sound a little strange that any man with a thousand acres should be bored ; but if he's poor and cannot go ahead and open up the land with several ploughs and a hundred boys or so to clear the farm of trees, bushes and rock, half his time he is merely waiting for the limited number of workers to finish the very necessary foundation jobs before he can make any real headway.

"Well," he said bitterly, pointing down to where John was trying vainly to plough a straight furrow, "there are many ways of making one's fortune, but that's the last thing I would do."

Bill was clearly trying to pick a quarrel, but I

wouldn't let him. Looking out over the landscape, which though it was in repose save for the rustling of the grass and the gentle waving of the miserable branches of a few dark trees, I felt would never impart peace to the heart of any White man.

"D'you see that stretch of land with that wood on it, over there beneath that hill?" Bill asked a little later. "Well," he smiled, "it was bought by a fellow I knew at home. He bought it about a couple of years ago from a chap he met in England, long before he came out. I thought that sometime we should be neighbours, he and I. Well, yesterday he came. . . . He only stopped a couple of hours, had a good look round then drove back again to Nymba in his Daimler. He won't come back again, he said so. Why should he? . . . he has no need to."

As we came round the bend we saw that Bill's men who had been digging up the weeds from his coffee-patch had evidently stopped their work. At sight of their master they hastily picked up their tools, looking rather frightened, for this was the third time that Bill had caught them idling. Bill suddenly lost his temper. "Clear out," he shouted at them, "you lazy brutes!" They did not seem to understand at first, and set frantically to work. Bill was a lenient master and the natives liked him, but now his face was red with anger. "Clear out!" he shouted once more, "and go to blazes!" The men had gone; they were running to their huts. Bill turned and looked at me and sighed. "Sorry," he apologised. "Oh, lord," and then he, too, walked away. . . .

# XXXIII

Our oxen and cows and a couple of calves were driven into their enclosure every night. This was a thick wall of thorn bushes, piled ten feet high, a *boma* as it was commonly called. The Masai slept in a grass-hut by the opening, so that in case of any raiders prowling round he would be ready with a spear. He was a light sleeper for a native, and once or twice thought that he had heard some footsteps in the night, as he sat by the ten-foot gate waiting to spring at the enemy. He was a brave man, that Masai, and always suspicious ; yet when a lion leapt into the *boma* to fetch a calf, he did not even hear it. Probably there was no sound. The calf was not eaten in the enclosure—the raider had carried off its victim before settling down to its meal. The Masai was greatly excited ; he was also slightly nervous. He wanted to borrow John's gun, for the lion, he knew, would be sure to return. The fellow had never handled a gun before—but that did not matter. A gun was magic ; the sight of a gun and a few loud bangs would be sufficient to frighten away any beast. Or so he thought.

"It will be a black night," observed the Masai. "The lion will not feel shy of his shadow."

He built himself a fire inside his hut, for company. John asked him to set the trap on the same spot where the lion had leapt over the " wall." There was no sense in letting him have a gun; besides it was against the law. The Masai did not sleep, he fed his fire till the smoke fairly blinded him, and then he sat and listened. . . . The dry sticks crackled in the fire, the crickets sawed and then Bill's dogs howled in the distance. When the fire had died down, the Masai cautiously opened the door of his hut and peered out into the dark for a long time. For a long time he saw nothing at all. The oxen did not seem alarmed, they stood swishing their tails and many were lying down. Uncertain whether he imagined it, he thought he saw a black shape which seemed to move only a few yards away. He quickly closed the door and sat motionless against it. Instinctively he grabbed his spear. Stealthily, slowly moving its tail, the lion crept to where he had leapt the day before—and suddenly was trapped !

The Masai heard it growl. The oxen heard it, too, and herded together frightened. The angry breathing of the lion and the rattling of the trap filled the night with horror, and then there was silence. Presently the Masai fell asleep. . . .

When dawn came the lion had gone—so had the trap. For two miles John and the Masai followed the tracks of beast and trap, but in the forest they completely lost them. This troubled John for days, for he hated cruelty. The Masai, contrary to John's instructions, had failed to chain the trap to a tree. Even so, considering that the trap weighed half a ton, it was astounding that the lion could have made good his escape. Once more John tried to track the beast with Bill's dogs, but they were no help to him at all.

# XXXIV

THE REFLECTION THAT ONE'S WHOLE LIFE IS BUT a short span of time, and that in a very few years one must face old age, begins to worry the exile long before his time. He feels that his true life is not really lived where he happens to be, especially if he is not successful. Brooding over this in the glaring sun at a hundred degrees in the shade, I leaped from my chair with pleasant anticipation as I heard that unusual and exciting sound—the cranking of a car somewhere in the distance. I could not yet see the car. Crank it went again and then again, and presently, oh joy, an antiquated Ford came rattling up the hill. It was cousin Jim ! Sitting beside him, in a pale-green frock, was the little governess.

" Hello, Joan ! " he shouted, waving his outsize hand through the sidescreen. " Jenny and I have just gone and got spliced." Jenny looked very happy. She was a dainty little thing, quite self-assured and surprisingly able to hold her own.

" There hasn't," Jim said, " been any rain for ten months in the outskirts of Nairobi " ; in fact the drought seemed universal.

" I thought we might as well get away now, until the weather breaks."

Jim was not unduly troubled. He was getting six pounds a week and a house built of sunbaked bricks, free. He was also due for a certain percentage in the profits—but so far there had been almost none.

"There will certainly be none this year," he announced decisively, " but damn it all, why worry ? "
From the back of his car he produced two bottles of whisky, a bottle of gin and a bottle of vermouth.
"Jenny likes a cocktail before dinner," Jim said.
He also unpacked three guns, so he was evidently going to have a little sport. Jenny, I soon found, took no interest at all in Jim's numerous sporting activities. Promptly Jim started to rebuild the damn. He rode our mules and with infinite patience he built a small boat, all on his honeymoon ! Jenny merely sat. She sat and stitched Valenciennes on to green crêpe-de-chine. She had already acquired that art of lolling of the tropics-condemned woman. She took elaborate care of her lovely complexion and never ventured in the sun before afternoon tea. Bill, too, came round of an evening and recklessly shared the cocktails, while his dogs sat at his feet and scratched. Jenny had brought a gramophone and a dozen or so fairly decent records. She had, I found, as the days went on, not very much to say. Jim, she thought, was " priceless " ; so was Marie ; so were John and Bill ; the cook and the dogs, and the books she read. Bill and John seemed years older than Jim, who was actually the eldest of the three. The drought and the ever-increasing overdraft were always on their minds. Silently they puffed their pipes, while they watched the antics of cousin Jim whose light-hearted behaviour did much to brighten the anxious days.
"Oh, God," I used to pray between laughter " let it rain . . . please don't let John fail." Between cocktails and gramophone records, in the middle of a party I had learned to pray. . . .
We often followed the clear and pebbly stream of an evening, an hour before sunset, Jim walking ahead

with the gun. It was the brightest hour of the day ;
guinea-fowls sprang up with a sudden tremendous
flutter of speckled wings, screeching and taking Jim
completely by surprise. There was the open field
on either side, parched and desolate. The land one
felt had no history, no human associations, and
slowly but surely it changed young men from
happy adventurers into hardened, callous, silent
plodders. . . .

Bill brought his mangy dogs along on these early
evening rambles, disturbing creatures though they
were, spoiling Jim's chances of bagging any kind
of game. Not that I minded, for I was absurdly
pleased whenever he missed a chance, not being a
sportswoman myself.

" I'd sell this seventh hell," I heard John remark
to Jim, " if only I'd get my money back. Profits
be hanged ! "

It was the first time that I had heard John really
speak his mind, and I knew he meant it. Nearly
five blank and profitless years had made it easier
for him to decide. He had given farming in Kenya
on a small capital a fair trial.

" I should sell out and go elsewhere," Jim answered,
after he had fired a shot into the general direction
of the swamp.

It sounded easy.

" I wish I'd gone to Canada," said John, " where
a chap can work, really work and keep fit."

We all sat down in the reeds, getting bitten by
insects. Every minute or so as Jim fired, a whole
multitude of birds simultaneously rose up from the
water, circling widely for a while, then dropping
down again to settle once more on the swamp. What
they found to eat I do not know, for I never saw a
living thing in the soda-impregnated water except

insects. The ploughed fields around were also alive with hungry birds, dotted here and there in flocks. A native collected the fallen birds and brought nearly eighteen of them—a dozen flamingoes as well as several puny wild ducks. Blazing into flocks like this seemed to give Jim a great deal of pleasure. But it required no skill. Slowly we went homewards again, the branches of the thorn-bushes and trees powdered with dust and ashes. Every now and then the dust blew skywards as the hot winds came thundering over the plain.

There was always this periodical feeling of a storm coming, but somehow we knew that it was a false hope. . . . To the north we saw the infinite distance, one range of flat-topped " elephant " hills behind the other. The whole world was brown-grey and dead. Once, long ago, it was fairly green, but never as green as in Europe. The rays of the sun slanted across the parched earth and then it grew rapidly dark. Jim swore at Bill's dogs, which spoilt his chances at bagging any kind of fowl. Bill was angry, for he was touchy about his dogs—and he grew angry so easily now.

Presently we heard a strange humming in the distance and then recognised the sound of an approaching tractor. Slowly it rattled over the rocky ground, a brand-new tractor driven by a native, on its way to our new neighbour, the ex-clerk. Silently we watched it go by, not entirely without a feeling of envy.

Next morning Jim went hunting in his Ford. He raced an eland for miles, recklessly disregarding holes and ant-hills. As he came within close range of the exhausted animal he fired a shot straight through its heart. It fell forward on its knees and then gently rolled over on its side. Its frightened eyes filmed over as the native took out his hunting knife to remove its head, for Jim was a keen collector of antlers.

Jim and John spent part of the following afternoon trying to get the ex-clerk's tractor going. Something had gone wrong. Something was forever going wrong as soon as it was left in charge of either its owner or his servants. Spare-parts in Kenya were not available except after many weeks of waiting. The natives had no feeling whatsoever for machinery, and things continually seemed to get broken.

On Sunday Jim and I went to the lake to launch his boat, followed by a bunch of negro children with dreadfully distended stomachs and ophthalmic eyes. Fed chiefly on badly-cooked maize and bananas, they suffered tremendously from indigestion, and looked sadder and far more serious than their parents. Rarely did I see a *toto* smile. Jenny was busy embroidering another set of underclothes and flatly refused to be tempted to go out in the newly-tarred and strange-looking contraption. She was also busy reading *The Sheik*.

We waded through the bullrushes, sinking almost knee-deep in the mud. Almost tenderly Jim placed his boat on the water, and very carefully we crept into its shallow bottom. It did not leak at first. The water was barely three to four feet deep but I shuddered to think of the appalling depth of mud below. Disturbing crowds of pelicans, we paddled gently towards the centre where a tiny island peeped above the water. Mosquitoes rose from their breeding-places, but neither Jim nor I were now affected by their sting. We were acclimatised. Jim tried to probe the depth of the mud, but found it beyond the reach of his oar. Arriving at the other border I saw something lying in the grass which aroused my curiosity. From the distance it looked like a sack.

P                                    225

Approaching closer, we saw it was an enormous python, moving slowly with that midday torpor of the tropics. Slowly the bottom of the boat filled with water and I urged Jim to hasten to the shore. I did not feel at ease ; rowing on a swamp was an over-rated pleasure. A giant tortoise came waddling through the shorter grass—the biggest I had ever seen. Jim promptly put the punt over it, expecting it to carry it, but the creature never budged so Jim had to carry it himself ! Untroubled as Jim was with an overdraft, with the anxiety of making a living, life also smiled on him in every other way. He had so far escaped malaria or any other tropical disease. Things, interesting things, happened to him, and he was never short of money. He must, I suspected, have received money from home.

There was a nest of bees beneath his now wooden bedroom floor, much to the annoyance of Jenny. He awoke one night to hear them buzz excitedly about the room, each ready to sting. Lighting the lamp to investigate, he found that a swarm of ants had driven them from underneath the floorboards. The bees were enraged. Even a couple of young snakes who unsuspectedly also lived underneath the floor were ousted by the ants. The battle went on for some time and then Jim went happily again to sleep, while Jenny lay fretting in the dark, tucking her mosquito net around her.

The same morning, at dawn, we were awakened by a most amazing hullabaloo which sounded for all the world like the booing of the mob in a play. This African world which was so strangely still at dawn now all at once was in an uproar. The voices sounded human . . . almost. Had the Kamasias at last made up their minds to kill us, and were they rushing our men and raiding our cattle at this very moment ? I went to the window but could see nothing. Cautiously I opened the door. Cousin Jim was already up, clad in his pyjamas, hastily harnessing the mule.

"There's a bush fire over there," he shouted, pointing to the west. " I'm going to see."

Off he made towards where the noise was coming from. It came and went : shrill, piercing voices emanating from the wood. The natives smiled and shook their heads. No, they said, they did not know what they were, but they were certainly not voices of men. They were sure of that. "Spirits perhaps," said an old man. Again the voices of the entire jungle seemed to rise simultaneously ; the dreadful sounds turned me cold. The Masai who slowly passed the house, leading the oxen to the plough, pointed to the distant fire which was threatening to destroy the wood. "Those are the voices of monkeys," he said, " they are very much frightened of something. The fire, perhaps." When Jim arrived by the wood the shouting had ceased. The fire had been checked by the stream. A solitary leopard slunk off behind some rocks. Jim fired and missed. A few baboons sat perfectly motionless, practically obscured by branches. . . .

The meeting had dispersed, and once more the world was still.

# XXXV

THE BLESSED LITTLE CHANGE THAT JIM'S VISIT HAD brought us was soon over. In vain did we try to detain him. "Soon," he said, "we are going home for nine months' leave, with pay!"

I went into the shed after he and Jenny had gone and sat down on his punt, which he had now completely forgotten. There were, I noticed, only fourteen sacks of maize left. I did not greatly care. Wild pigeons were cooing on the roof and mice scampered into their holes. Once more we were left to our own uninteresting lives. Once more Jim hooted his horn as he disappeared over a rise, and then the silence was profound.

"Five years," I sighed to myself.

I felt like an old woman who lives in the past, talking to herself of what once has been. By and by I heard John shouting at the driver. He was down below on the plain, ploughing, barely disturbing the surface of the sunbaked earth which should have been rich and green with shooting corn. Beyond the plains, where the swamp merged into the yellow grass, the hills were brown and bare. A party of young native girls, practically naked, were marching single file down the narrow path. They giggled and seemed merry. By the pigsty they squatted down for a moment whilst one of them removed a thorn from her foot. Presently they passed the shed, but did not see me. They were unwashed, and the odour of their bodies lingered long after they had gone. " This is not Tahiti," Jim had once said, when eyeing some native women at work. . . . Below on the giant plains, over the stony waste places, a couple of ostriches paraded proudly. Presently a native arrived with a note stuck on to the end of a bamboo stick. He held it out to me from a respectful distance and then promptly sat down in the dust. It was from Bill.

" Let's go on *safari*," he wrote, " and all else be damned. What's the b—— use of waiting for rain anyway ? "

" All right," I scribbled on the back of his note.

A change, I felt, was imperative. John, too, was willing and told the half-dozen or so remaining fellows we now had left to be ready next day at dawn to carry our loads and accompany us for a week's trek into the wilds. A slightly dilapidated tent which Jim had also left behind, was packed. Bedding, camp-beds, crockery, pots and pans, a change of clothing, food and ammunition were tied into bundles weighing about sixty pounds each. The cook and the houseboy both came as well, so did the cook's wife, for he did not trust her to be left behind.

We met Bill at daybreak by the elephant-path, which led up the steep bit to the escarpment. He was going to walk. John and I rode our mules, taking turns with the child in the saddle. When we arrived at our starting-place, I was amazed to see a dozen or so native-women lined up, pregnant some of them, ready to carry the loads up the steepest part of the journey, while the men were going to walk behind, carrying nothing at all.

" Why," I asked the women, " don't you refuse to do your masters' bidding ? "

" Refuse ? "—from the one in front. " Refuse ? " piped another from behind. They looked at each other and then laughed.

" *Memsahib* does not know," said the oldest, who was probably some fellow's mother, " that women are stronger, much stronger than men. . . . Men," she smiled, " their limbs are like grass."

Remembering the self-same women applauding the warriors at the dance I was somewhat puzzled. The men who stood behind me, mute and slightly hostile, each carried knobkerries tucked into their belts. That effective weapon, which could nip any would-be argument in the bud. After a steep climb lasting half an hour we arrived on level ground. The women handed over their loads to the men and returned to their huts and babies, shouting merrily after their husbands, who took no notice of them at all. Happy women, I thought. Bill said so instead, making disparaging comparisons between the White man's and the Black man's method of giving their women what they needed.

" Let's have a look at Kenya from a different angle for once," said John.

" From without, so to speak," said Bill.

" The explorer's angle," said John.

" The writer's angle," I thought.

" The b—— Capitalist's angle," added Bill, and laughed.

We trekked for many hours through elephant grass as it was called, which was, in truth, tall enough to conceal an elephant. Presently we came into a rocky region where the grass was short and shadeless. Flat-topped trees abounded. The only wild flower I saw for years, apart from a few water-lilies, was a flowering red cactus which John discovered after four hours' trek. It bloomed alone, as though it had strayed from another country.

The natives talked and sang, but presently they grew tired and kept silent. Ours was a poor sort of outfit, not like those of the professional hunters, Government officials or other rich people who brought along their baths, cane chairs, gramophones and other twentieth-century luxuries. After a rest at midday we came to a forest, a wild, primeval forest it was. Frequently branches had to be chopped down to make room for us to pass. Progress was slow. There was silence in the tree-tops as we passed, not a movement we saw, nor a single creature. Kamau the houseboy said he'd seen dozens of colobus monkeys silhouetted against the sky. We barely believed him, but the cook said he had seen them too. The eyes of natives, we realised, were better-trained than ours.

Again we came to a clearing where the grass was green, and there was water everywhere. My mule almost disappeared in a swamp, as I rode him ahead of the outfit. After that there was more forest, more dodging of branches and thorn-bushes. Trekking on and on at about ten thousand feet above the sea-level, our tempers were none too good ; in fact we were run down, the three of us. Marie was crying for milk. Bill and John, who took turns on " Ginger," did not speak at all. We crossed the stream and Bill's boy dropped his bundle in the water. It was Bill's bedding. . . . Bill flared up and hastily gave him " the boot behind," which later he regretted.

We were now high above the world, having climbed steadily up to thirteen thousand feet to get a glimpse of the most stupendous panorama. It was stimulating to think that we were on top of the world and far away from any creeping city. We could look upon an empty world below, crags leading down and away into another plain, in which no man had settled as yet ; a world so unfamiliar, a wilderness as yet unvisited, walled in with bare escarpments as well as forests. After a while we met a pioneer-wagon laden with bedding and a table, two White men following the outfit and two negroes—all looking very tired. They did not even glance at us. It was clear that they had no wish to stop and talk. They had been gone many tedious hours by the looks of them and to judge by the geography of the place, and were now " speeding " along to the right towards a river and were soon out of sight.

There were signs of other earlier travellers having gone the same way towards the river : there was the sun-bleached skeleton of a donkey at the side of a path, and a human skull nearby—White man or Black man, we could not tell. The remnants of a wagon were embedded in the limpid stream, abandoned in the end like so many efforts. . . .

In a little clearing encircled by the eternal thornbushes, a dozen or so negroes were gathered together, palavering over a camp-fire. They jumped up as they saw us, looking slightly guilty, as though they had gathered together for no good purpose. They were friendly enough as we talked to them, but looking back, I saw a packet of salt—my salt—change hands between my cook and the strangers. I saw him pocket a coin, a silver coin. He had not sold it cheap.

Unexpectedly, to our great surprise, we came upon a White man's camp. Two almost new bell-tents were peeping cheerfully from beneath a cedar tree. But there was not a sign of a soul. All our natives stopped and stared. A packing-case covered with a sticky-looking table-cloth was laid for someone's tea ; two battered thick plates, two knives and forks and two tin cups were laid at each end of the table. There was a blue enamel teapot, too, which had seen better days. Something else, covered with flies, was in another, a tin plate. It looked like bread left over from the week before last. Flies were everywhere, some were dead, stuck on the cloth or on the jam pot. Two canvas rocking-chairs stood on either side of a packing-case which had evidently been used as a writing-table, for on it were an ink-pot, a drawing-board and some pens. The tent flaps were closed tightly.

We were just moving off when two men arrived on foot, and stopped us. One was completely bald, which came rather as a shock as he looked quite handsome before he had removed his topee. He was middle-aged with a flat, florid face and did not look the kind of man who would be able to stand that altitude for long. They were very glad indeed to see us, and the bald man talked and asked innumerable questions. The other, a young man, kept silent, though occasionally he smiled. He was the sort that one felt one liked straight away. . . . We were pressed to stay for a cup of tea. " *Mpishi*," the older man shouted for the cook, who was nowhere to be seen. I saw him rapidly crawling on his stomach from underneath one of the tents, trying to escape from the back, as he had evidently been asleep on his master's bed ! Some more cups were presently brought from a box, ex-railway cups they were with a pale blue crest on each, and very much chipped.

The two men, who were working for the Government surveying the land, having already spent three months in the open, were tremendously glad to have someone to talk to. We were the first White people they had seen. The older fellow talked incessantly ; his memory, considering he lived in Kenya, was splendid. He could not bear the talk to flag, even for a moment. There was nothing he did not know on any subject, and what he did not know about Kenya was simply not worth knowing. He passed judgment on everything with the most enviable cocksureness and possessed a store of statistics which we, who were silenced, had neither the chance nor the knowledge to contradict. We had never met a man so versatile.

The young man only smiled and listened ; it was enough, we liked him. His boss was telling John and Bill how to run their farms, fairly revelling in our and other farmer's problems, and was able to solve them in a jiffy. His theoretical knowledge of farming was amazing.

Tea was being served, but the pot was disappointingly inadequate, and there was no sugar. Condensed milk was dribbled from a tin, a few drops into each cup. It was a melancholy sight to see that tin turn black in less than a second with swarming flies. . . .

" Help yourself to bread," said the elder man, passing round his mouldy loaf. We were not very hungry. There was some apricot jam in a tin on the floor which was temporarily neglected by the flies, which seemed to find preference for Nestlè's milk. There was no conversation, only a monologue. " Bring some biscuits," he shouted to the houseboy, who unobserved had also crept out from the other tent.

" Biscuits *naquisha* (finished)," the boy said resignedly. They had been *quisha* for ages and all that was left in the storeroom now was a tin of Sanatogen.

Our host was telling us that some months ago he had been camping in a dry river-bed in a particularly wild part of the country. The boys, who evidently knew better, had lain down to sleep on the bank. Suddenly and unaccountably, in the middle of the night, a stream of cold water came rushing down from the distance, filling the empty river-bed with a torrent of water eight feet high. For a whole week the water thundered past and he, who had just managed to rescue himself, had been left high and dry on one side of the river while his boys and his provisions were on the opposite side ! They could not get across for days. Yes, for nearly a week he lived on porridge. . . . It was all there was on his side of the water. He had never liked it since.

He had also shot an elephant the week before last —at least he thought he had. They were out looking for game when they came across two elephants : one was grazing in a swamp nearby, while the other one was standing in the shade of a tree. They were beauties from all accounts and had the most amazing tusks. They decided to kill the one under the tree and both men fired simultaneously. Their aim was good and the beast fell dead. The young man, who wanted to bag an elephant for himself, decided to go and look for the other, which had in the mean-while disappeared. Both men lit their pipes, resting against the dead elephant, examining his valuable tusks, and then they went off after the other. They could not find him. After about an hour's search they returned to the one they had killed, " but would you believe it, he was not there." Apparently it had only been stunned !

The two men did not want to let us go, and very

nearly made up their minds to come with us, although we had not asked them. We rode out into the silence and tranquillity once more, none of us speaking a word for hours. Solitude of long duration made you silent. . . .

We came to a half-circle of bamboo-bushes into which a leopard had just disappeared. Bill had always wanted to bag a leopard-skin for his mother, and his idea was that we should surround the leopard and chase him out into the open.

" If we stand over here," he said, " and you on the other side, while the boys beat the bushes from behind, he is bound to come this way. All we have to do is to have the rifles ready, and to fire."

The cook who was an unusually good shot and a keen one, planted himself between John and Bill, whilst the natives started to beat. They carefully approached to where we were, and then suddenly there was a low growl, and instead of a leopard, a lioness faced the cook ! He saw her first, and it was up to him to fire the first shot. Luckily, he forsook his gun and took to a tree nearby—the only tree within half a mile. Bill, who spotted the lioness a moment after, shot her neatly through the head. The cook might not have aimed so well, and the situation would have become dangerous. We did not want to lose our cook, for more than one reason ! Needless to say the other natives laughed. It was a blow to his dignity, and he did not think it very funny. Away, across the level of the flat escarpment, a speck had disappeared like lightning, it was the leopard. We almost doubted whether the experience were true, so quickly had it happened.

There was the dead lioness being skinned most

scientifically by Bill himself, and I couldn't help wondering if her mate was far behind. . . .

It was nearly dark when we stopped to camp. The tent was pitched in a sheltered spot and the cook placed a couple of empty kerosene tins upon an open fire and hastily made a few scones, boiled the water and presently we had tea. A card-table stood unsteadily in front of us, our chairs were much too high and things were being spilled. We were still feeling very cross. Our tempers, I noticed, did not really improve until we went down to a much lower level. The high altitude affected us and we felt easily exhausted, had touches of headache and attacks of giddiness.

Barely had the cook opened the tin of condensed milk when our camping-place was swarming with flies. This was surprising, considering that there seemed nowhere on this vast plateau from where they might have come except, perhaps, a carcass or a corpse. They covered the meat, drowned themselves in cups of tea and tried to enter our mouths. We barely slept that night. It was not restful sleeping in the open. To lie " under the stars " is anything but soothing or romantic. We were cold, too. I listened to the sounds without and wondered how I managed to sleep so well in Mannington where the tramcars rattled beneath our windows.

It was at dawn, when we were driven from our beds by ants, that we had a sudden vision of indescribable glory. Almost unbelievably beautiful, Mount Kenya rose out of the mist like a mirage. Like a sentinel it stood above a lonely world. . . . Feeling altogether brighter and greatly compensated, we trekked towards the north, coming upon several wild pigs which stampeded over the plain, throwing up the dust of burnt grass so that it resembled a black tornado.

Both men fired and missed. One of them swore. Indeed, swearing had become a habit of late. . . . For three days we trekked with absolutely nothing of interest happening at all. We ran short of meat, of bacon and of bread. The cook fermented flour, sugar and water in a bottle by corking it and placing it in the sun, thus producing the most effective sour dough. Over an open fire he turned out half a dozen loaves with the greatest of ease. John shot a kongoni, which greatly pleased the natives. First and foremost they cut the carcass open to snatch the entrails which, still warm, were considered a delicacy.

We saw a rare sight the following day—rare even in Kenya. A herd of elephants was feeding by a swamp far below in a valley. There were thirteen of them. Shortly afterwards we met a rhinoceros. It stood quite still, and then, contrary to what one expects of a rhino, it turned and walked away. Luckily it was indifferent to our approach—otherwise some of us might have been killed. The natives did not seem unduly frightened ; they were a merry crowd and picked up their sing-song barely a second after the beast had turned away. I had a great liking for these natives, and I think they liked us, too. I am convinced that there was not one amongst them who would not have given his life for us. Apparently never much surprised at anything, taking every possible thing for granted, I have seen them only genuinely amazed once. It was not the first aeroplane by all accounts that took their breath away and filled them with awe ; it was not really the big things which caused them to marvel. It was the little things. It was, in fact, the first soap-bubble Marie blew which almost caused a riot. . . . A perfect bubble floated gently towards the houseboy as he came round the corner.  Wide-eyed, he stood for a second or two and then fled.  Others came to see the miracle ; they, too, did not like it.  It was " supernatural."  The houseboy ran to his hut, closed the door and became slightly hysterical. . . .

## XXXVI

STILL EIGHT THOUSAND FEET ABOVE SEA-LEVEL,
the air was cool. It was an uninhabited world,
giving one a feeling of complete desolation. Since
the beginning of the world the place had seemed to
have been untouched by time. It would, one felt,
pass on thus in all eternity. For days we had not
seen a single path made by human feet. How small
the overwhelming loneliness made one feel ; this
wilderness, how unimportant. Again we pitched
our tent, still within view of Mount Kenya,
which looked strangely out of place in its surroundings.

The natives as usual built a bonfire which was
designed to keep wild animals at bay, and long after
we lay in our beds they sang and talked. Presently
they started to pray, according to their various creeds.
Natives, I knew, loved praying loudly and in
public. Mohammedans, Nonconformists, Catholics
and Anglicans. The Nonconformists as well as the
Anglicans usually sang a well-known hymn or two,
rather out of tune ; the Catholics, two of them,
recited the Rosary with serious, quick-tongued
urgency. The Mohammedans prayed visibly, but in
silence. I was stirred as usual in the night with
strange uneasiness. I never slept on *safari*. Trekking
in Africa does not create that " delicious sleepiness "

one would expect. One is disturbed by insects and strange sounds, whilst instinctively one is alert. The sluggish forms of the sleeping natives lay in the darkness beside the fire. Marie and John, as well as Bill were fast asleep. I might have been the only living thing in the midst of this strange tranquillity. Eventually I, too, grew drowsy, but presently the rock rabbits (hyrax) began their ecstatic love-song. It sounded not unlike the crying of many children. There seemed hundreds of them, crying louder and louder, till they reached a pitch of hysteria almost human. Weird though it was, it seemed companionable.

At dawn the wind slightly changed, and again I wondered if perhaps it might bring rain. . . . There was not a cloud, but I fancied I heard a kind of murmuring, an undercurrent of sound, like distant thunder. In the early dawn the highlands of Kenya are friendly and undeniably beautiful. Gone was the strange hostility of the night before. After a breakfast of sizzling kidney we packed up again and went still further north. John burst into song sometimes ; occasionally Bill joined in. There was, I found, no need to talk. Still I heard that murmuring sound, but as usual did not trust my ears. Unbelievable though it sounds, about noon we saw a rainbow in the sky ! This was not trickery, the others saw it, too. There had not been a drop of rain for twelve months now, yet there ahead of us was a rainbow, and we were coming to it !

" I wonder if we'll find a bag of gold," said Bill.

" What's that ? " I asked the cook, pointing to the rainbow.

" Magic," was all he said.

Q                                      241

"Can you hear anything?" I asked him a little later.

"Yes," he said.

"Well, what is it?"

"Water," he answered simply.

The sound was getting more distinct as we advanced. It gradually grew into a roar. It was (as we began to suspect) an enormous waterfall. We came to a wide river which dropped with amazing suddenness into the abyss below, apparently almost into nowhere. An invisible whirlpool sent the spray heavenwards, to be caressed by the magic rays of the sun, thus creating an everlasting rainbow.

"By jove," shouted John, "this is worth a bag of gold."

We promptly decided to stop, although the natives did not like the place. They did not like the rainbow; it was something they did not understand. Camping by that river, as well as our vision of Mount Kenya, was a never-to-be-forgotten experience; one of those experiences (which one can count on the fingers of one hand) which stand out in later life. The "sunny bits," as Bill called them. It was not a "healthy" spot to camp by, being too near the drinking-place of animals and too close to the jungle. Before sunrise, when the cook brought us our early cup of tea, he shouted above the roar of the falls that a lion, a big black-maned lion, had just slunk off. He had seen it nosing round our tent, inches from where we lay.

"It can't have been hungry for human flesh," grinned the cook. Outside, on the sandy ground, were its footprints—on my and Marie's side of the tent. There was a gleam in John's eyes, and Bill was already shouldering his rifle. . . .

Pretending they were going for a stroll they disappeared, secretly following the lion's tracks. I was profoundly grateful when they returned two hours later " without success."

" Where have you been ? " I asked, as though I had not guessed.

" Oh, just messing about," Bill answered casually.

I was afraid to spent another night in that tent, but did not like to admit it. Yet it was, I thought, unfair to the child. Recalling stories I had heard of people being fetched out of their tents by lions, my imagination fairly ran riot. . . . We were in turns eaten by lions, lost in the bush, dying of thirst, charged by rhinos, trampled to death by elephants and bitten by snakes. . . .

When I looked into John's shaving-mirror, I thought that I already looked years older.

We were again short of meat and something had to be done about it. After several vain attempts, Bill shot a wild duck which fell into the river. We had had no meat and no vegetables for two whole days. Bill was getting frantic. Hastily he removed his shorts, jumped into the river to rescue the fallen bird. It floated too close to the waterfall for my liking, for smooth though the water looked, there seemed a strong current down stream.

I called out to him, but he could not hear me above the roar. It was the most awful moment of my life. . . . I felt convinced that he would be carried away into the abyss. The water was not really deep ; indeed, I had seen a herd of zebras cross the river just where Bill had jumped. Slowly the puny little duck was carried down-stream, Bill following behind with even strokes. He was a good swimmer and he was not going to let his bag go. It was as if his whole life depended on rescuing this tiny morsel of flesh. Eventually, almost breathlessly he grabbed it and slowly swam to the shore, which seemed to take him a long time. His face was ashen ; he was trembling and could barely get his trousers on. It had been a very dangerous thing to do and certainly not worth the trouble. Once the bird had been plucked, it was no bigger than my hand. Bill lay on his bed for the rest of the day, feeling rather sobered. He could not keep his teeth from chattering nor did he want to eat the bird ; his appetite had gone. Diving into the cold river had brought on an attack of fever. . . .

John had a sanguine conviction that if he waited by the stream until sunset he would easily secure a buck. A herd of at least fifty zebras approached the shallow drinking-place and gradually crossed to within a few yards to where we lay in hiding. John did not shoot, for in the distance several eland approached, as none of us cared greatly for the flesh of zebra. But they seemed to sense our presence and suddenly fled as if pursued—just as the eland were crossing the water. Startled by this sudden panic they, too, disappeared except two which came so close that it was difficult to take good aim. Even killing through sheer necessity seemed cruel when one is so close to a creature that its heart can be seen pumping with fear. It seemed so much more natural to chase one's prey. . . .

I sat by the camp-fire that night, wishing that I were back in Mannington. I watched the moon slip behind the escarpment, until it left our little camp in complete darkness. . . . Shadowy black figures were squatting behind the cook's fire reciting : " Hail Mary, full of grace, blessed is the fruit of thy womb." Thinking of the lion which would probably return, I felt none of that lure of Africa one can hear so much about. I would have much rather camped by a Derbyshire moorland stream—yet even if my wishes could come true, I would have much preferred to lie in safety within four walls, between soft sheets in a big, wide bed with Marie safely at my side.

## XXXVII

Bill, WHOM I HAD DOSED WITH QUININE AND WHO was now very restless in his bed, called :

" Do you know, Joan," he said, " that when we came through that green swampy part two days ago, after we found that cactus, I suddenly made up my mind about my future. I don't know why I should have decided just then. . . . I'm going to sell my farm—if I can, that is ; and then I'll go to Somerset or Devonshire or even Cornwall, where there are meadows with flowers in them, and clouds in the sky, and where the air is fragrant. I'll keep pigs or fowls or grow violets, and I'll work like blazes . . . shan't care about profits so long as I can just keep myself."

Bill was silent after this surprising outburst. Perhaps he fell asleep or maybe he dreamed of the romantic charm of the country he had so happily left, where fruit trees stood in bloom now, where season followed season in exquisite changes of colouring. Bill had changed his mind, but then he had changed it long ago but tried not to admit it to himself. Ever since he had left off finishing his new home he seemed to have known it was no good. By and by John, too, crept to his narrow folding-bed, placing the rifle by his side. The cook, faithful soul, came round to pile up our camp-fire and then sat down by his own with his head between his hands. His wife was asleep, her woolly head resting on her arm. On the table lay some newspapers which Bill had received from home about a month ago, a small provincial paper. In it was a picture of a lady laying the foundation-stone of a chapel, at the same time handing a donation of a hundred pounds to a clergyman. It was marked in red pencil. . . . The lady, I noticed, was Bill's mother.

Waiting until I had retired, the cook sat by his glowing embers. He then came across and squatted outside our tent with John's shotgun placed across his knees. There he sat until dawn, and then he brought us cups of tea. The loyalty of his race, I felt convinced, is something the White man does not honour as he should.

" *Memsahib*," he said, " the lion did not come. Lion not hungry for White man."

Bill came crawling to the breakfast-table with his forearm bandaged and covered with blood. He smiled rather apologetically.

" Good heavens," I cried. " Bill, what have you done ? "

" Oh, nothing," he replied.

He had, he told me after breakfast, been awakened with a burning pain in his arm. Lighting the lamp, he noticed two red spots on his arm which looked suspiciously like snake-bite. Possibly, he thought, he had been bitten by an ant ; but as he could not be certain and did not want to die just yet he took his penknife, cut the flesh criss-cross and dropped a tablet of permanganate into the wound.

" I'm quite all right now," he added, " but let's shift camp and go further north. This darned roaring gets on my nerves."

It was, in fact, the altitude which caused much of our uneasiness ; none of us could stand it. It had a peculiar nerve-racking effect. Looking back as we departed, we saw a column of luminous spray rise upwards through the air into the sunlight. We saw it still when we came to a bend nearly an hour later.

Far below in another valley which lay hot and brooding in the midday sun, a small oval lake lay dreaming, surrounded by trees. It beckoned irresistibly. A klipspringer on the rocks below uttered a piercing cry and disappeared. A placid giraffe which stood grazing heard the warning cry and galloped away with lurching, comical strides. Eventually John discovered an elephant-path down the side of the escarpment, which we daringly followed. My mule was inclined to stumble, so John and I changed mounts. Omera, a carrier, who was a Catholic, crossed himself several times and kissed the crucifix which glittered in the sun, as it reposed against his navel dangling from a string.

" What's the matter, Omera ? " I asked.

" I'm frightened, *memsahib*," he said, looking at me with his big brown eyes. " That water," he went on after a while, pointing to the lake, " is magic. It is witchery. It is not a lake, not a real lake." Omera perspired profusely, his voice was husky with suppressed excitement.

" What do you think it is, if not a lake, Omera ? " I asked.

" It is an eye, an open eye."

" Whose eye ? " demanded Bill rather harshly, as though he was determined to get to the bottom of this nonsense.

" An eye of God," whispered Omera. " You see," he went on after we had walked another half-mile or so, " it has no outlet, no water flows into it from anywhere. It just is . . . unfathomable."

Down we went to where a herd of golden-brown antelope fled in panic ; they had just been drinking by the lake. Omera stood still and then suddenly dropped his load, saying that he had heard the voice of a honey-bird twittering in the woods and he felt obliged to follow it. He would be back again, soon. Odero, the Mohammedan, shrugged his shoulders as he picked up Omera's load and said : "He's afraid of the water. I, too, do not like it. Maybe we will perish if we go too near."

The other boys held back at some distance and one by one dropped their loads. They would not approach any closer. A bed of blue-white water-lilies covered part of the dark and silent pool—looking for all the world like a carpet spread out in the sun. John, who got to the shore first, tore off his shirt and, to the horrified amazement of the natives, plunged into the water for a swim. A sacrilegious act! Bill, too, removed his clothes and, completely forgetting his last night's malaria, he dived head first into the lake. The water was clear but bottomless, apparently, and very cold.

"*Memsahib*," said Odero gravely, as he came up to me, "maybe the *Bwanas* will now die . . . maybe they will have many misfortunes."

Stripped of clothes as both men were, it was evident that both were not as healthy as they should have been, or as they once were. Both were far too thin for one thing, whilst the colour of their skins was yellow. Misfortune, as far as we were concerned, was ours already. The natives squatted by their loads. They were thirsty, but would not drink (as we did) from the water of the lake. There was, as they said, no visible river or stream flowing in or out of this miraculous " eye of God." The pool was strangely still. The natives, too, were silent and there were no birds. Affected by the superstitious, awe-struck natives I, too, felt the place was haunted. But John and Bill did not share this belief. " By jove, that was grand ! " said Bill as he donned his helmet. . . .

There was a strange light in the ascetic-looking face of Omera when he returned. He picked up his load without uttering a word and stood waiting. The natives seemed infinitely remote from us at that moment ; they were at all times closer to the earth, the trees and the jungle. . . . We went down into the valley which was like a furnace beneath the blasting fire of the sun. It was quite possible that no other White man had ever come along this way before.

# XXXVIII

$A$S IF SOMEONE HAD PRODUCED HIM OUT OF A HAT, a Vaderobo came upon us in the centre of the plain ! He was a shrivelled old nomad, with a wild prophetic look in his completely crazy eyes. He salaamed and then, true to custom, spat. He pointed to his stomach and then he looked up to the sky and opened his toothless mouth. He was hungry, he said, and had grown too old to hunt alone. Many an elephant had he killed in his time whilst he had thought nothing of fighting a lion single-handed. Now his children and his grandchildren had turned him out ; they did not want him any more ; he was, in fact, *de trop*. He had followed our outfit from the waterfall. Odero, our linguist, translated the old fellow's rigmarole.

The Vaderobo's old and bony hand trembled and shook his spear. We forthwith called him King Lear. He was greatly pleased when we invited him to join our *safari*, and before nightfall was greedily eating the almost raw meat of a young zebra. He sat apart from the rest of the men, in the outer circle of the firelight. He did not sing with them, nor did he pray.

King Lear was not an attractive native, he was shifty and grovelled in the dust. The Vaderobos are a roving tribe of sorcerers, living entirely by their wits, never doing a stroke of work and never owning, or wishing to own, a single thing except perhaps a dog or two. Too lazy to build themselves proper huts, they haunt the woods and bury themselves in hollows and caves like rabbits. They also frequently die like flies from perfectly preventable diseases. Many of them were blind, caused through ophthalmia. Often they starved when their luck was out ; whilst children first were sacrificed if there was not enough food for them all.

They suffered untold horrors and privation, yet they calmly preferred death to any kind of work. Too lazy to cultivate the land, they stole if they could from others, and if likely to be tracked down by the authorities they hastily abandoned their hovels. They never could be found. Like the deer of the forest, they sensed the approach of the enemy before he was at hand.

" Vaderobos not much good," said the cook. " Low fellows, very low fellows," he added contemptuously.

We were now down again to about three thousand feet above sea-level and were being stung by tsetse flies. This was a new experience so we decided to go back. King Lear, too, had now had enough. He said good-bye with a deal of spitting and gesticulating and turning of eye-balls. The last we saw of him was his frail body, clad in a fluttering loin-cloth, fading away up the scorching buffalo-track, carrying a load of zebra-meat on his back and being followed not only by swarms of flies but by vultures in the sky !

Eventually we arrived in the Kamasia country, where the heat was as intense as in the Simba valley. Steam-jets squirted from the ground, proclaiming the tropical hell it was. A shallow lake lay drowsily in the midst of the dreary landscape ; it was alive with thousands of flamingoes. A hippopotamus was sunning itself, looking blissfully contented and almost coquettishly ducking its fat and shiny body beneath the water at the approach of our *safari*. We camped by the lake which was named after an Anglican bishop who had once, long ago, been murdered by natives. Suspicious Kamasias approached aggressively, yet with the utmost caution. They sent a " delegate " to open negotiations whilst some of the tribesmen watched and spied from behind bushes. One of our carriers, a Kikuyu, was the only one of the party who understood their language. He said the men had come to offer their hospitality, which included a bucket of milk (a present from the chief) and the pick of their women for our men, including Bill and John. Bill felt horribly embarrassed and looking at me, blushed. John thanked the delegate very politely ; he also tried to spit—but his efforts were not very successful. He also asked them what we could do for them in return.

They did not want much, they said. A dead hippopotamus was what they wanted most. Pointing to our guns they implied we should find it easy enough to grant their wish. Presently we walked into the tiny village, disturbing their fowls, and had a look at the primitive huts and even more primitive women. Caked with mud and cow-dung, covered with flies, thin and shapeless as they were, our men kept chastely to themselves. Not that they were particularly fastidious as a rule.

One of the villagers had an array of arrows spread outside his hut which had been dipped in poison, which he kept in an old tobacco-tin. Poison was the only thing the natives seemed to draw from nature. Of the curative qualities of some of their herbs they knew absolutely nothing at all. Considering every native had this store of deadly poison, it seemed amazing that they did not kill each other, in the course of their frequent arguments. A little scratch— and all is over. A silent pact perhaps, an unspoken law, fear of witchcraft—whatever it was—they possessed the most brotherly spirit of *laissez-vivre*. One of the natives said he owned a kind of treasure, a "pitcher" as he called it. He was going to show it to us later on. It was almost like a ritual, for in the evening he came along and slowly unwrapped several layers of bark, removing them tenderly. It was only a photograph, "a picture," which he held proudly upside down. They all held it upside down, I noticed, or sideways. Still it was a photograph, the White man's magic.

Many years ago, the proud owner said, a passing Dutchman had taken it, during an epidemic of rinderpest. It showed a whole herd of dead cows which his grandfather had owned. The Dutchman had given his grandfather a copy of the snapshot and there it still was, handed down like an heirloom from father to son. It was very much the worse for wear. Bill made a copy of it for me to keep.

After two miserable days and nights spent in this mosquito- and fly-ridden valley, John bagged a hippopotamus. We could not in honour have departed without displaying the magic of the White man's weapon. We left them gorging hippo fat and quarrelling over its hide. Were these, I asked myself as I waved good-bye, the warlike and bloodthirsty savages of yesterday ; the men of whom I had been so afraid sometime ago? There they stood, about a hundred of them, clad in a hundred rags, as friendly as any other tribe. Our own natives had kept rather aloof. Were they, I wondered, snobbish like the White man ?

The chief, who came with us part of the way, looked no different from the rest. A shade more intelligent perhaps, that was all. Pointing to the sky, he remarked : " There will be no rain for another five months at least. . . . Many men will starve,

but not we Kamasias ; we never starve." Their cattle
very nearly did, I thought, as I saw them feeding off
the strawlike tufts of grass.

Back again in the Simba valley we were met by
those strange spirits, Kavirondo cranes. Following
us, circling above, they squawked and lamented in the
most depressing manner. Approaching our isolated
mud house with its shiny iron-roof, I felt that it had
an air of friendliness and welcome. I felt as though
I had returned to a homely shelter with at least a few
happy associations. I was indoors again and it
seemed less lonely, less desolate than the wilds. The
carriers, too, were glad to be back ; so was the cook
and his footsore wife. She was looking quite pert
again, after what was to her a week of incredible
boredom. The spiders had survived in the meanwhile
amongst the rafters, so had many other homely
insects. The lizards resented our early return, having
taken possession of the sideboard.

# XXXIX

LOOKING OUT UPON OUR FARM AS WE SAT ON THE verandah was very depressing for both John and myself. Luckily, so far, John had had very little time to think. He had been ploughing and clearing the ground from morn till night. He had sown again and yet again. There had been work and more work, but his high hopes had not materialised—there had been too many disappointments, losses, mosquitoes and flies, and too little rain and too little money. He was feeling old and in doubtful health. He had so wanted to believe in this dream; but now, having grown wise before his time, he was forever thinking of ways and means to make a change. . . .

Bill came round more frequently now. Almost with apprehension he asked :

" Do you think there is a ghost of a chance for me to sell my place ? "

His farm was less developed than ours whilst there was his half-finished house, like a ruin telling its own tale. Both our farms were now on the market : it looked pretty bad. Our store of maize was nearly exhausted ; and soon there would be no food left for our men, and no money to buy any more.

Exactly a fortnight after our return, both our mules became sick and died. The cause, so the Masai declared, was a disease caused by the sting of tsetse flies. We had, on our journey, passed through a fly-infested area. We had all been stung, but had not been aware of the danger. . . .

After the seventeenth month of drought I was just recovering very slowly from an attack of dysentery when a strange herd of emaciated cattle arrived, driven by another Masai. The owner had sent them to us to recuperate—not that we had more or better grass than he, but he put his faith in our saltlick. It was indeed remarkable to notice the gradual change in the animals, considering that there was nothing for them in the way of food from which to pick and choose. They seemed to subsist on salt and water. Kenya seemed to have given us one asset, the salt-lick. Twice daily, entirely on their own, the oxen and cows roamed towards it, for another bout of self-indulgence.

The owner of the cattle himself arrived a few days later. It turned out to be a most eventful day for us and for him too. He was a tired-looking man of thirty-five, and he rode a tired horse through a tired valley. Eccles was his name. He had once been a lawyer, but like us and many others had been romantically attracted by the lure of the " open spaces." He had left his office and exchanged it for a " place in the sun." Now he had all the sun he wanted—and more ! Towards sunset, after he had ridden off by himself, for he was a very shy man and unsociable, he returned, rode his horse up to the doorstep and called into the dining-room where John was sitting writing letters :

" I say, I think I'll buy your place ! What will you take ? . . . I don't want your coffee and I don't need your ploughed land, all I want the place for is my cattle. I wouldn't live down here for anything. . . . I'll give you a thousand . . . no more."

We were speechless for a moment. I immediately

grew extremely anxious, lest he should change his mind. . . . A £1000 it was and we were glad to get it. Indeed, it was almost too good to be true. We weren't going to lose our money after all—not all of it anyway !

My rose-tree lay ruined over the edge of the verandah, its roots were bare ; but it did not matter now. Our period of waiting for rain was suddenly over. We were going to retreat. Those mere scratches that our plough had made were soon to be weed-ridden again. Buried our acres would be in no time, and covered with weeds—like some forgotten grave. The abandoned house, the store and the mill would again become a refuge for snakes and rats and insects. In less than six months from now there would be no trace of our six-year sojourn. How much I had come to hate the Simba valley, I had not realised until now. . . . It had taken so much and given nothing in return. It would now revert, almost at once, to the savage state we had found it in. We had wrested from it less than a bare living. We had harvested not a moment's peace from it, that peace the farmer in England is bound to reap, though perhaps his profits, too, are small. The drought, we knew, had been a blessing to some farmers, big men who had enormous stocks of maize stored away. To them the old stuff had been worth its weight in gold. . . .

" Honestly," said Mr. Eccles as I showed him our bedroom, hoping to sell him our furniture, " I'm uncertain whether I have done right buying this place. An hour ago I was debating with myself whether to go back home to England and live on £250 a year, or to go in more extensively for cattle-breeding out here. What do you think ? " he suddenly asked of me. What did I think ? I did not tell him. . . .

No, he did not want any furniture—a bed perhaps, in case he might stay a night occasionally ; and that dining-room table of yours, I'll have that, too. He gave me five pounds for it ; it had only cost me three. This was the best stroke of business which had yet come my way since we had lived in Kenya ! There was also a box full of cyanide on top of the wardrobe with which we could have poisoned half the country. John had bought it to kill rats and mice and to poison thieving leopards, but somehow had never used it. Heaven knows why, but Eccles had that too. For a little while he stood in front of my wardrobe which we had bought second-hand and which had a full-sized mirror to it. I don't think he had seen himself reflected full-length for years ; the man that looked at him from the mirror quite clearly shocked him. Impulsively, he bought that too. . . . That mirror had reflected many a negro since I had it and it had been quite usual for the cook or the houseboy to lead their guests into my bedroom when we were out and to let them have a thorough look at themselves !

Eccles' younger brother was coming out from home in a day or two.

" It is rather a responsibility," he said.

This was partly the reason why he bought our land. He wanted to expand, to try his luck with dairy farming. Up the valley, ten miles from Nymba, where he had lived and where he had bought three thousand acres four years ago, cattle did not thrive for any length of time. Even coffee, he said, did not bear as well as it should ; he found that the trees produced only half the quantity of beans than in some other places. It was difficult, indeed, to know what to do. . . . Sometimes he had wondered whether he wouldn't chuck it all—but then one couldn't go back somehow ; besides, what was there to go back to ? Anyway, he was going to see the lawyers in Nairobi when he met his brother there, and finally settle the matter. I prayed fervently that he would. As he was peering short-sightedly at everything with his pale blue eyes, he looked the most studious farmer I had yet met. There may have been no need . . . yet I felt exceedingly sorry for him.

Poor Bill, we hated to tell him of our good fortune ; but he took it very well. He looked at Marie as she played a game of ball with the houseboy, speaking Swahili to him with an amazing flow of words. She was a very weedy girl now. " I don't know how you have stood it so long," said Bill. That was all. Bill had now ceased to pretend, to me. He, too, left the valley later, after his family came out from England to pay him a visit—a trip which cost his family far more in cash than Bill had originally set out with to make his fortune. We sent our furniture and implements, our oxen, wagon, buggy and plough to be sold at Nymba. We knew that we should never come back again. There were exactly seventy acres of ploughed-land waiting below in the sun, the fruit of five and a half years of labour. It had not given us the security we hoped, and it promised absolutely none. . . .

We were returning to the old kind of life, and our dream-world had faded away. It was said that the price of land in our valley was going up, owing to the demand. The " demand " having been created entirely by us, Bill, the man from London and the ex-clerk ! The place, so it was said, was getting populated.

Once more I made the round of the farm, caressing the mill, the store and other ingenious contraptions which John had so cleverly constructed. We went to say good-bye to the natives. . . . The new master was taking them over next day. A huge Swahili had come down the day before to look over the place. He was going to keep an eye on the coffee trees after all, scanty and undersized though they were. It would have been a pity to let them deteriorate.

" *Kuaheri* " (good-bye) our natives said simply, but they did not smile.

Gravely they accepted some of our blankets as parting gifts, but there was no sing-song that night and not much talk.

The cook came flip-flapping to the bedroom door next day with his enormous flat feet, bringing us for the last time our early cup of tea. Everybody had left in the night, absolutely everybody, he announced with glee. The Swahili rang the bell as the sun rose over the hill, but no one answered its call. The farm was deserted ; gone were their goats and their chickens and their small private potato patches were stripped of produce. Filthy rags and other rubbish were lying about everywhere. They had wrenched things from their fittings : pieces of wood, doors and fences. Desolate it looked and ramshackle.

" They not like new master," said the cook. " He not smile, he look like a hawk." I gave the cook my wrist watch as a farewell gift—it was all I had to give. He was absurdly pleased, unable though he was to read the time. It was " alive " as he said ; it ticked.

" You come back from *Uleia*, White man's country, and I will cook for you again." He did not believe that we were not coming back. No one believed it. One always came back, they said. " Africa never let you go ! "

But we felt no lure. Many, we knew, came back because they had to. Once more I shook the cook's hand—and then off we rattled over the ruts in a borrowed Ford, and I felt free. An appalling dead

THE LAND THAT NEVER WAS

weight, which we both seemed to have carried about with us for years, dropped from us all at once. Fear and anxiety had gone ; we seemed to have stopped to take breath. As we rolled over the bumpy mud-road, sunbaked and dusty, we almost felt tempted to look back once more . . . but we didn't. What would have been the good ? Kenya had blessed us with one decent crop of maize in five and a half years, that was all. Why look back now, upon the bare, unlovely plain ? The road was still in bad repair ; no one seemed responsible. A few bridges were evidently going to be built—soon. The bleached skull of a steer lay on the road-side, long picked clean by vultures. A motor-tyre with a broken rim lay beside it, a testimony of someone's laborious journey. It had once been buried in the mud.

# XL

W E PAID THE HOTEL-BILL AT NYMBA, WHICH HAD now been owing for two years. The manager was slightly drunk ; by his side was a bottle of whisky and his shîrt was minus a collar. He seemed to be almost offended as he took the cheque and examined it. He would have, one felt, gladly entertained his guests, or his friends as he called them, for nothing. " We are going home," I said, " for good."

" For good ? " he repeated, looking at me rather queerly.

" For good ? " he said again. " Well," he suddenly shouted, " let it be for good, and don't for Christ's sake come crawling back with the mistaken idea that now you have no other choice. Don't let your own country lick you, never mind about this ! It's not too late for you—didn't I tell you though ? " he went on angrily. " Didn't I tell you that it was no damn good ? It's cursed, that's what it is, cursed ! Might as well gamble your money away in Monte Carlo as out here. Much better . . . much healthier."

" Mind you," he added after another drink, " you should have taken my advice. That plot of land, you remember, in the centre of Nymba, I was going to let you have cheap—well, I sold it last week. I'm hoping, when I've sold my other two plots, to go home as well, and stay there."

Bullfrogs croaked again in the gutters of Nymba ; the manager, grown much older, completely bald now, his face a sickly white colour, had yet another drink. . . . Old Mac had died three years ago and was now buried in Nymba's cheerless churchyard.

I also went to pay the doctor's bill over at the hospital. It was a very modest bill, for we had learned to do without doctor's aid. The doctor sat at a desk in his consulting-room, thinner than ever, looking deeply absorbed, studying an account book. Five or six negro patients stood about the room. Presently each received a tablet or two of quinine, which they chewed with relish, and then trooped out. I had brought my medicine-chest with me which I was going to leave behind. Practically all the bottles were still intact. Healing the natives, as I did all those years, I had needed only three things : quinine, Epsom salts and disinfectant. The doctor offered to pay for them, seemingly very pleased to have the stuff.

" I'm feeling very generous just now," I said, " because I shall not need it any more, as we are going home."

The doctor removed his coat, for the heat was almost unbearable beneath the iron roof. Through the inner doorway I saw a tiny little garden, some attempt at a rockery and two rose-trees all but withered and covered with dust. Natives passed in the glare outside, swathed in bandages and smelling of lysol.

" Well," said the doctor, " don't get downhearted if you every now and again get an attack of malaria at home. You've been here far too long at a stretch, all of you. Don't . . . ah, well, what's the use of a lot of advice ? Anyway, don't look back now and think of the years ' the locusts have eaten ' ; it's no use, no use at all. I often think . . . it's the ' afterwards ' for those who go back, how they live after, which would make interesting reading." " Yes," he said again, as he shook my hand, " it's the ' afterwards.' " He sighed, " I wish I could go with you."

The bank manager and his wife were at home in England on leave, so were several Government officials we knew. Freddie, too, was back again in Abyssinia for another stretch of " penal servitude." He had, so the hotel manager told me, bought one or two useful plots of land which looked as if they might prove promising. " He's not such a sissy as he seems," he added.

The priest, I heard, was still alive " by the Divine Grace of God " and had started yet another mission.

About midnight, as we boarded the train at Nymba, some shadowy creatures walked up the pitch-dark platform, and grabbed John by the hand. Some of our Kikuyu farm-hands had come to say good-bye once more ! They were going home to their reserve. The Masai also joined us a little later. He had been with us over five years and had hardly spoken more than a dozen sentences all that time. He, too, was going home to his reserve.

" Who," he asked, " is going to mind your cattle in England ? "

We were not going to have any cattle in England, we said.

" No cattle ? "

It was evident that he thought it a poor sort of a place. . . .

It may provoke a smile of amusement or even disgust among the hardened farmers and old-timers, but I must confess that I had no other regrets at leaving Kenya except having to part from the natives as we knew them. Willing, cheerful, loyal and trusting as they were, their memory will always be dear to me.

The sun-glazed Indian Ocean gently lapped the coral-reefs of Mombasa as we stood by the golf-course watching some holiday-makers from the uplands, having a half-hearted game. A change down to sea-level was the best thing if one could not go home, but even for that we had never had the money. Once more a boat had arrived *via* South Africa ; our boat, bringing a few returning officials, a few farmers and once more a handful of young hopefuls. Once more John scanned the horizon—it had become a habit with him—but still there was no rain. . . . But it did not matter now.

We were obliged to spend the night at one of Mombasa's oldest hotels which lay on the outskirts of the little township, high above the sea. There were other people there also waiting for the boat, a strange assortment indeed. By the table near the door sat a family of four, who appeared to feel ill at ease as none of them spoke a word either to each other or to anyone else. The father, a little man with an old-fashioned moustache, ate almost everything with his knife. " That little chap over there," said a Scotchman who was also waiting for the boat, " is now a millionaire. He came out before the war with a trunk full of goods, and now he owns one of the biggest stores in the country. He had sense, that fellow, as well as foresight. Scotchman, of course," he added proudly. He himself, a born farmer, was going to work at home in future. " I like work," he said, " and can't stand natives doing it for me. I have gone slack," he added, sadly pointing to the flabby muscles of his arm, " and I don't like it."

An oldish man who was sitting on our right was continually and with loud voice finding fault with the Swahili waiter.

" Look here," he shouted, " what's the meaning of this ? " pointing to a morsel of cork which was floating in his Burgundy.

The native, dignified and polite, begged his pardon and brought another glass. This time the glass was evidently not quite clean, and again the waiter was shouted at, and again he politely fetched another glass.

" Dirty swine," said the White man to the room at large, " they want teaching a lesson or two."

The silence for a moment was profound. The waiter stood at attention by the door, his face as expressionless as a sphinx.

" It's a funny thing," remarked a commercial traveller who had been trying to sell a very cheap line of tasteless women's clothes in the hope that the native women would buy them (but had evidently done badly, as most of his samples, apart from making but little appeal, being too small.) "It's a funny thing, when you come to think of it, but I never came across a native who was without dignity."

It was a happy-looking island, all kinds of coloured people were lounging on the quay, watching the boat go out to sea.

" The lazy swine," said a lean and nervy-looking Englishman, as he watched them lounging about by the gangway, smoking cigarettes. He said it with conviction. He had been in Kenya for many years, but somehow he had not yet learned to laugh. The natives were chatting furiously among themselves, laughing at life—and who knows ?—laughing at the White man and glad there was not much to do, existing splendidly on the minimum of labour.

One gentleman was seen off by his servant, who wept quietly at parting. The servant himself had also brought a servant with him, his own. He could well afford one now, especially as his master was paying him his wages until he returned in six months' time. It was the servant's servant who carried most of the luggage.

It was the same colourful island that we left behind, with the same blazing sun beating down upon it, the same busy life in the streets, the same babble of many tongues, the same pale green clusters of palms —a place that knew no poverty. But to us it appeared in a different light as we drifted out into the Indian Ocean, seeing it fade away behind the horizon. We had left something behind, but we knew not what. . . . But I know now—it was our youth.

The Indian Ocean was rough. Some passengers, a few only, stood on deck looking back, the rest went quietly below. What did they care about Kenya's receding coast when they were going home at last ? It was a most uneventful journey, most people keeping to themselves. There is a different spirit in a boat that is homeward-bound from one sailing from England. Experience, ill-health and the mixed joy of going home to a place which would never be quite home again either. . . . A whale had followed the boat for several days and some small birds had settled on the masts hundreds of miles from the coast. The Captain, a small man and very thin, walked about with a continual frown to ward off inquisitive passengers. He was not an easy man to speak to, and hardly anyone ever tried. One lovable lady-missionary patiently painted a little water-colour for me, the sunset on the Suez Canal. She, being very old perhaps, had more faith in things than any other person on the boat. She also passionately believed in the progress of Christianity amongst the natives of East Africa. Two precocious and anæmic children, born in Kenya, were on their first trip to England and were greatly amused at seeing White people doing manual labour, and doing it better and working much harder than any native servant had ever done. A couple with three children were travelling back home after six years in Tanganyika, where they had been trying to grow tobacco. They had lost almost all their money, whilst their two partners who had stayed behind had long gone off to prospect for gold, but had not been heard of since. Their youthful enthusiasm had been sadly misplaced, and now a knowledge of failure was theirs which was most distressing to see.

A cold raw mist enveloped the Atlantic as we neared the Channel. I wrapped my overcoat (which was over six years old) around me. The coat was sadly out of fashion, as was John's best suit, whose jacket reached half-way down his knees. A young man standing near me, whose contract of four years in the Malay States had, owing to the slump, finally come to an end, was starting his first cold. He had, he said, exactly five pounds between him and the doss-house. . . . Two fine-looking policemen waited on the quay-side, and were passionately envied for their jobs by more than one young man returning on that boat. . . .

## XLI

Back again in the old drawing-room of John's childhood with its flowery chintz elegance of a by-gone age, with Dante meeting Beatrice over the bookshelf, and " Wedded " over the piano—our African venture already belonged to the past. It seemed as if we had only dreamt it, and as if the world had long stood still. An enormous coal-fire had been lit in the old-fashioned grate, although it was only the end of summer. But we were both shivering with cold and my temperature was slightly up again. It had been drizzling all day, and the air was raw.

Later in the evening the guests who had been invited to give us a welcome home arrived. Aunts and uncles as well as cousins, all looking a little older, all very much surprised we were not in love with Kenya, none of them having the faintest idea what we had gone through, were full of their own little affairs and minor ailments. No one was much interested really, nor did they genuinely care. We, who had hugged the fire, were ousted from our places on the hearth-rug by the older members of the family.

" Tell us all about it," one misguided aunt had asked us brightly.

They had been a well-to-do crowd ; they still were. They grumbled a good deal and talked of economy although they had never known a moment's hardship in their lives. They still strongly advocated emigration—for others. Their theories were wonderful, but wildly off the mark. John refused to talk about his doings of the last six years : never to this day has he spoken of them to anyone. In many ways it was a pity, for lacking imagination as well as information, our elders formed their own opinions and judged us harshly. It was just our two selves against the family. . . . We had suddenly become of no account, having failed to return with our fortunes made. Sitting quietly in a corner, we sadly realised that we had also lost the gift of small talk.

As we crept to bed in order to keep warm, I felt that they might at least have left us our places by the fire. . . .

" If they weren't happy out there," I heard a voice from the cloakroom saying, " they should have been ! Not everybody has a piece of land, a thousand acres, at their disposal, to just do as they like with. Mark my word, they'll regret leaving. . . ."

**THE END**